# LIVING PARABLE

Chet Lowe

# LIVING PARABLE

Copyright © 2016 by Chet Lowe

Book Editing & Interior Page Design by: Maritza Cosano
Maritza@littleredrockingchair.org

Cover Design by: Jordan Sharp

ISBN-13: 978-0-9968501-0-0

Living Parable
www.livingparable.org
Email: questions@livingparable.org

Give feedback on the book at:
questions@livingparable.org

Printed in U.S.A

# Contents

With love to
my wife, Andrea, and our children,
to Barbara Lundy who inspired me to write, and the cowboys in
Okeechobee who listened to the stories as I wrote them.

# Foreword

Jesus' parables are timeless. Inexplicably, they are unbound and alive to the hearer in every generation. Most of us have read at least one of the parables of Jesus—wonderful stories that are capable of conveying biblical truth in a way that cuts through time periods, social differences, intellectual understanding, age and culture.

Jesus was asked a simple question by His disciples in Matthew chapter 13 as to why He spoke in parables. "He replied, 'Because the knowledge of the secrets of the kingdom of heaven has been given to you, but not to them. Whoever has will be given more, and they will have an abundance. Whoever does not have, even what they have will be taken from them. This is why I speak to them in parables: 'Though seeing, they do not see; though hearing, they do not hear or understand'" (vv. 11-13 NIV).

Some people don't grasp the full meaning of truth when it comes only in written or spoken words. They need to see it, touch it, smell it, taste it, and live it experientially. That, dear friend, is where I would like to introduce to you my brother, fellow pastor, gifted teacher and friend, Chet Lowe.

Occasionally, God places someone in your life who is so uniquely gifted by the Lord that Ephesians 2:10: "For we are His workmanship, created in Christ Jesus for good works, which God prepared beforehand that we should walk in them," comes alive before your eyes. Someone so unique, you can see the imprimatur of God's eternal plans in their life and that the phrase, "God made a one-of-a- kind piece and then broke the mold," fits not just the person but the God-given calling of that person's life.

*Living Parable* is an example of what a life looks like when it actually lives out the teachings of Jesus—experiencing a life lived in total abandon to a central truth—to know God and make Him known.

In studying the biblical parables, we can easily see they illustrate some of Jesus' most important teachings. They demand crucial responses from us, just as they did from those who first heard them. In order to gain the greatest benefit from the parables, we must understand what they are and how they function. To that end, a parable is an extended metaphor or illustration. It is an illustration turned into a tale, which is elaborated on the spur of the moment by a gifted teacher.

Jesus was accustomed to preaching to a crowd with a wide range of understanding and attitudes. He based each parable on common, every-day events that made up first-century life—lost money, sheep and shep-herds, and cruel creditors. Like most illustrations, parables usually have one central point. And for Jesus, that focal point was His coming kingdom.

This book is kingdom-focused too. It is the story of experiencing Jesus' principles every moment of every day, living abandoned to the King. No cost too high, no mountain too tall, and valley too low—it is a "Living Parable."

The kingdom in the Gospels does not have to do with a physical terri-tory or realm ruled over, but with the rule or authority itself—God's rule on earth in the person of Christ. Jesus demonstrated that kingdom author-ity over disease, demons, nature, and supremely over sin and death. And in His teaching, preaching, and parables, He revealed the standards and values of the kingdom.

These contrast sharply with the values and standards of our contem-porary Western society. Just as the parables of Jesus brilliantly illustrate important truths about Christ's kingdom, and present to us truths which demand a response, so I pray this book will illustrate for you what a king-dom life looks like lived with abandon for the glory of God. The sad fact is that in our world—even in our churches—selfishness, rebellion, and sin often close our minds and hinder our response to the truth of the Bible. I pray that as you read this book, you will be touched in a profound way to reevaluate your own commitment to living a life abandoned to the cause of the kingdom of God and you will be led, challenged, and encouraged to respond to the call of God upon your life.

We are living in perilous times. The hour is now for every believer to rise up and live out what we profess to be true. May your life too become a living parable.

Pastor Jeff Gill
Senior Pastor, Calvary Chapel South Bay

# PREFACE

## Let Go of Your Lawn Chair

*"But he said to me, 'My grace is sufficient for you, for my power is made perfect in weakness.' Therefore I will boast all the more gladly about my weaknesses, so that Christ's power may rest on me. That is why, for Christ's sake, I delight in weaknesses, in insults, in hardships, in persecutions, in difficulties. For when I am weak, then I am strong."—2 Corinthians 12:9-10 (NIV)*

I have discovered that life is meant to be an incredible adventure with Jesus. With each step and every breath we take, He is there guiding and directing our path in order to conform us into His image. Every situation, experience and circumstance is divinely purposed to mold and shape our being so that we can shine as a light and give all the glory to our Father.

Sometimes the process is not so glorious. Still, He tells us to "trust the Lord with all of our heart and lean not on our own understanding." I am sure that the apostle John came to this conclusion as he wrote his divinely inspired Gospel account. He said, "These are written that you may believe that Jesus is the Christ, the Son of God and that believing you may have life in His name" (John 20:31).

While John did not fully understand during the earthly ministry of Jesus, he surely got the message as he wrote down the seven miracles, and the evidence of his changed life is recorded in history. The truth is that Jesus has an adventure for you.

Your purpose is to glorify God, and His desire is to give you an abundant life. The Scriptures record that we are "living epistles" for others to watch and follow. Our life story reflects God's glory as the plot of our existence unfolds for the world to see that He is alive as He works through His people. This adventure makes us living parables put on display so that the church can be strengthened and the world can find their Savior, Jesus Christ the Lord.

# LIVING PARABLE

It is hard to believe that Andrea and I have been married for twenty-one years. I remember praying twenty-five years ago for a beautiful, blonde, Christian woman who would be willing to surrender all and follow after Christ. The Lord gave me my perfect complement, providing my heart's desire! I praise God that He knows exactly what we need and meets that need according to His riches and glory, and not our own.

Andrea truly is "my heart," as the lovers of Song of Solomon call one another. She is gentle; I am not. She is faithful; I struggle. She is steadfast; I waver. She likes operas; I do not. We do have a yearly escapade to New York to watch a Broadway show, as well as watch her dance down Fifth Avenue singing, "I love New York."

She is simple; I am complicated. Nevertheless, she respects and honors me in a way that constantly makes me feel like the most important man in the world. Andrea is a beautiful visual of the love of God for my life, as He has given me more than I could ever hope or imagine. For this, I am grateful. To celebrate our anniversary this year, Andrea and I decided to return to the place where our love began to take root. In the most important moments of my marriage, I have always found the first three chapters of the book of Revelation—which exhorts the church to listen, take the words to heart, and act—to be an exhortation to my marriage as well.

Just as John writes to the church in Ephesus that though they had works and labor, they had left their first love; I find that in many marriages, even my own, it is easy to do the same. As couples, we get so busy with life, children, careers, and even church work that we forget to nurture the very person with whom we are to become one—our spouse.

Because of this tendency, Andrea and I went back to our special place to reminisce, to remember the love that founded our relationship, and give glory to the Lord for all He has done in our lives together. It was truly an amazing night! It began with me teaching a young adult discipleship group.

Andrea and I decided this year to spend our weekly date nights (which have turned into date days) in ministry, and then take some alone time to talk, laugh, and enjoy life. It was late by the time we left, so we got into the car.

# PREFACE

"What do you want to do?" I asked.

Typical of Andrea, she asked me, "What do you want to do?" Then quickly added, "Let me tell you what I was thinking and see if it matches up with what you were thinking."

She loves games; I do not!

I already had in my mind that I wanted to take Andrea to the park we frequented as newlyweds. I had even mapped out how I wanted the evening to play out. I would take her to Walmart to purchase cheap lawn chairs, stop at a sub shop to buy her and my favorite subs (an Italian and a roast beef with provolone) and go to the park to sit and talk. For the first few years of our marriage, we did this on a monthly basis for one of our date nights. It was cheap, but they were the best! Besides, we were putting two students through college on a teacher's salary; it was all we could afford.

The park, situated on the New River in Fort Lauderdale, Florida, is peppered with mossy oaks, a few scattered palm trees and surrounded by multi-million dollar homes. With each passing yacht, Andrea and I used to sit and dream of what would never be our reality. I must admit that at times I wrestled with the familiar covetousness as people waved to us from their boats. But hey, I had my girl, my lawn chair and a sandwich. What else could I want in life?

"I want to go to that park," Andrea said with much delight.

Exactly what I had in mind.

"We're married!" I said, for this concurrence pointed to that very fact. We both laughed our way to Walmart where we bought each other our anniversary gift—lawn chairs! After purchasing the subs, we found our spot in the park and as we watched the yachts passing by, we began to talk about the memories we have made over the past twenty-one years. This moment together was sparking in both of us that first love that is so easy to forget in the fast pace of our lives.

We reminisced about our experiences during the war in Liberia, counted the fifty-three children (outside of our own) who have lived with us since we have been married, and jokingly concluded that we must have Post Traumatic Stress Disorder because of the war.

# LIVING PARABLE

We were so lost in conversation that we did not even realize the late hour, and that we were the only ones left in the park. While we sat there, we noticed army helicopters flying over us in some kind of drill they were doing at the Fort Lauderdale port. This only made for more laughter, as we remembered being helicoptered out of the war in Liberia, and then, brought some tears as we thought of the horrific trials we have endured for the strengthening of our faith.

Peter makes this very clear in his first letter to the dispersed church: our trials will perfect, establish, strengthen and settle us (1 Peter 5:10). Oftentimes, I do not understand the Lord's methodology, but I am always grateful for what it produces.

"I wonder if we will be here twenty years from now," Andrea said as she looked around our surroundings.

"With how our life goes, I don't know if we will even make it that far," I said, and then we laughed, because it seems we are proof of Murphy's Law, which says, "Anything that can go wrong, will go wrong." It was at that moment that Andrea's eyes bugged out of her head, as she looked beyond my shoulder. I turned quickly to see what she saw: a young man, about six feet two, briskly approaching us from the woods in the park.

From our angle, he looked like a modern-day Goliath with blonde hair. And from the size of his bulging biceps ripping through his tank top, he obviously spent a lot of time at the gym. I could not see his face until he was about fifteen feet away from us, but when I finally got a closer look, it was obvious that something was wrong. I had seen this kind of face before on the child soldiers in Liberia.

He was angry and seemingly frustrated. If I could have seen into the spiritual realm, I would have said he looked demon possessed. However, my eyes were fixed on his right hand. Down by his side, as if to hide what he was holding, I thought for sure I saw a knife.

There was nothing we could do! Before we knew it, this young man was upon us, and I sensed that familiar feeling of fear in my heart. Trying to act as if nothing was wrong, I fearfully yet cheerfully said with a cracked voice, "Hey man, what's up?"

# PREFACE

I look back and wish I would have confidently said, "Get thee behind me, Satan," or "I rebuke you in the name of Jesus." The problem with fear is that you begin to rely on yourself and not on the God who says, "Do not be afraid for I am with you."

My voice arrested him in his tracks about five feet away from us. He glared at us for a moment (though it seemed like an eternity) and then quickly walked behind us toward the road. Andrea stared at him as he marched away.

"Leave him alone," I said, interrupting her thoughts. Then, I turned as Andrea watched him take the knife and brutally stab a palm tree that was about fifty yards away from us. At this point I said, "Jesus just saved our lives."

Suddenly, he took off as if he had seen a ghost. I believe he saw an angel holding a flaming sword, but I will only discover this truth when I reach heaven's shores!

Stating the obvious, I said, "We need to leave."

"Yep!" She said.

"Give me the lawn chair," I asked Andrea, as we walked out of the park and quickly tried to come under the streetlight. It's amazing how light gives us security. I'm convinced this is why the Word tells us to walk in the light, as He is in the light. In this, we find safety and security.

"Ah, that's okay," Andrea said lovingly. " I can use it as a weapon if he comes back." Andrea is all of 105 pounds when she is soaking wet, and I am sure that he would be very intimidated by a woman of this stature accosting him with a LAWN CHAIR! We laughed at the thought of her using this chair for her protection, but inside, God was speaking to me to release my own "lawn chair" and trust in Him. I walked toward our truck cautiously, almost expecting the young man to jump out of the bushes. Thankfully, there was no other incident, and we were able to drive away silently and somewhat in shock over the event. I felt as if I had just been in a car accident and was experiencing all of the visceral and emotional upheaval that happens in such a crisis. About three minutes down the road, Andrea burst out laughing.

# LIVING PARABLE

"Muma, you do have Post Traumatic Stress Disorder." I confirmed our earlier conversation. Let's face it, other women would have been freaking out about now.

"You're right!" She said as she chuckled, but I realized it was much more than that. Andrea was settled, established, and strengthened because of all the trials we had been through. For her, this was simply another story of God's grace in our lives. For me, it was another reminder of my weakness perfected solely in Christ's strength. After all, what did a fearful greeting and a lawn chair do to ward off this evil attack? Only the Lord stood with us.

Those previous statements are key to the context of this book. For it was earlier that very same evening that Andrea had turned to me and said, "What one thing have you learned in the past twenty-one years of marriage?"

"I am a weak man," I said without hesitation.

As we drove home, I further emphasized that I had come to realize that all that has been done, all that will be done, and nothing can be done without Christ in me, the hope of glory. Truly, apart from Him we can do nothing! The event only confirmed to me the reality of our faith.

I would rather boast in my infirmities, "For when I am weak, then I am strong." These are the words of Paul in 2 Corinthians 12:10. Jesus made it clear to the apostle that in his weakness Jesus would be strong. Embracing weakness has been a lifelong lesson of faith. In this alone, Christ is magnified and the church is edified.

Truly, there is an adventure of faith for you. The same Spirit that empowered ordinary, weak men in the book of Acts, wants to use you today. My prayer is that as you continue to read, you will be inspired to trust the Lord for all the steps of faith you are to make for His glory. He asks you simply to follow. I guarantee you will look back at the end of your own story and say, "To God be the glory; great things He has done."

# INTRODUCTION

Growing up in a denominational church, I remember my Sunday school teacher detailing the stories of the Bible in many different ways. Whether we dressed the part, made clay figures of Noah's ark or colored pictures of David and Goliath, the truths of Scripture were being planted in my heart and mind.

As a child, I likened those caricature drawings I made into Crayola masterpieces to the cartoons I watched on Saturday morning. In essence, they were fantastical, make-believe stories that were for mere babysitting purposes, while it seemed my parents were really learning about God in the adult service. Still, God used the truths of His Word in those pictures to penetrate my heart. I desired to hear the voice of God like Abraham, to save a nation of people like Joseph, and live the adventures of Elijah and Elisha, the great prophets of God. Yet, I was unsure if these stories were only to be read about in the Bible or if they were examples of what a believer could anticipate living out each and every day.

There was nothing more incredible to me than to know that God rescued the three Hebrew boys from the flames, saved Daniel from the lion's den, and caused Peter to miraculously escape prison. I listened intently to the adventures of Paul's journeys by land and sea for the sake of the gospel.

I heard Jesus say that He had an abundant life available, and I decided to live His quest for my life. After all, if Acts is the only inspired, recorded history of the church, I figured that it must be a model of what we can expect in the Christian life.

Going to church was great, but living church was what I wanted. Jesus introduces us to the living church as He describes the kingdom of heaven in Matthew 13: "The kingdom of heaven is like...." Jesus takes the time to explain heavenly principles, referred to as parables or heavenly truths, in a common understanding, or common language.

# LIVING PARABLE

In Luke 17, we see how Jesus later on in His ministry begins to further explain the heavenly kingdom, as He says, "The kingdom of God is within you." He explains some truths of the kingdom in the parables of Matthew 13, and then He says that the kingdom of God is within you. Now, Jesus wants to express that truth through us.

We are living parables.

Looking back, I can say that God has been faithful to allow me to be a part of the living church, but now I pray to be a living parable. In fact, my prayer is that each person that reads the pages of this story will be inspired to be living parables themselves. Just like the life of the prophet Hosea illustrated God's unconditional love for His people, God wants to write a story of faith that proclaims His work in our lives as a witness to the world around us. Our experience with the Lord becomes a living parable to spur others on in love and good works, as we press on in faith despite our failures or successes.

God has an adventure waiting for you. These adventures of faith are written not for you to tell, but to inspire you to develop your own.

# BULLETPROOF BIBLE

*"Follow my example, as I follow the example of Christ."*—1 Corinthians 11:1 (NIV)

*"Join together in following my example, brothers and sisters, and just as you have us as a model, keep your eyes on those who live as we do."*—Philippians 3:17 (NIV)

## 1982 - 1983

"If you don't receive Jesus as your Savior and Lord, you are going to go to hell!" This statement may seem slightly harsh, but it is the simple truth. As a seven-year-old, it was the clearest way I could get across to my friends that they were in need of a Savior. I could not imagine anyone would want to forsake heaven. Therefore, after attending a Billy Graham Crusade I thought to myself that if Billy could host a crusade, so could I.

My mom tells me the details of how I would prepare our garage for a neighborhood crusade. I would tell stories from the Scriptures using flannel boards, (really dating myself at this point) as there were no iPads or computers available for my presentation. In fact, the most exciting technological advancement known to man at that time was Atari's Asteroids game (now I am really dating myself).

The stories of David and Goliath, Daniel and the Lion's Den, as well as Jonah and the Big Fish would fascinate my friends as they listened in the heat of my garage. All the while, the Lord was stirring my spirit with these feats of faith to discover this God who provided such incredible adventures in this life. I knew then I wanted this kind of faith and would settle for nothing else!

I know this direct approach may not seem to be the best way to go in our world of political correctness. However, it is out of the mouth of babes that we could probably learn a thing or two about the need man has for a Savior. Although my techniques may have matured in presentation over the years, I pray the simple truth will always remain the same as when I was seven years old. We are sinners. We need a Savior. Jesus died for our sins and rose again on the third day. We need to receive the gift of God in Christ Jesus in order to be saved.

Our mission is to preach this gospel to every nation. In no way is the truth harsh. It saves! What is harsh is an eternal destiny separated from Jesus. From an early age, I knew I wanted to tell people this truth. My parents had purposed to raise me in the Lord and would provide opportunities for me to grow in grace. Whether it was family devotions or prayer, going to church seven times a week, being a part of Boys' Brigade (the Christian version of Boy Scouts), or setting an example for me to follow, they chose in their hearts to dedicate and commend me to the Lord for His purposes in my life, and not their own.

Every year, our local church would host a missions conference in which we would participate. Over the course of the week, there would be many events designed for the sole purpose of spurring the body of Christ into missions work around the world as supporting senders or becoming missionaries.

With great intrigue, I would watch the Wednesday night prayer service for our missionaries and wonder if God could act even though we were so far away from those that were serving around the world. I would hear people sing old-time hymns and anthems with such force that you would think the walls were coming down.

In fact, my dad's favorite was #423 in our hymnal, "Wonderful Grace of Jesus." Every "Favorites Night" at the conference, he would have me raise my hand to ask for that number to be sung. These conferences would etch wonderful memories into my mind of the power in prayer and praise.

Throughout the week, various missionaries would be invited to church homes to share with smaller groups the works of God around the world. Each year, I would sit in my home and listen to missionary after missionary share their story. There were miracles, healings, supernatural events, and most importantly to me, people were getting saved. However, there is one story that I will never forget.

The evening was much like every other time we had hosted one of these events at our house. Around seven o'clock, people from our church would start trickling in and filling themselves with various food items my mom had prepared earlier that day. It seemed the favorite of our denomination was tuna fish sandwiches with the crust removed, cut into quarters since they seemed to be at every event, wedding, or funeral that was hosted at our church.

My responsibility was to open the door every time there was a knock or the doorbell rang. As people were talking and laughing, I remember running to the door to answer a very faint knock. In fact, I was not sure if it was a knock at all. When I opened the door, I was surprised to see an older Asian couple standing on the other side.

"Is this the Lowe house?" They asked politely in broken English.

"Yes, please come in," I said, equally polite, though I couldn't help but stare. After all, I grew up in the Bahamas, had immigrated to the States, and had never really seen anyone from Asia before. The older couple moved slowly and people rushed over to help them with their things. I wondered why everyone was making such a big deal over them, and did not realize that they were the guests of honor until they began to share their stories later that evening.

I was disappointed. All of the missionaries I knew were Americans. They had left their homes of comfort and gone around the world to sacrifice themselves for the sake of another culture and another people. "Go into all the world and make disciples" had a tangible, physical visual in my eleven-year-old world, and this older couple did not embody my perceptions. I had no expectation of hearing any kind of adventure from this weak, feeble couple that sat before me.

The older Asian man began our meeting with prayer. It was obvious that English was not his first language. He had a very heavy Chinese accent and seemed to struggle to find every word. My impatience began to grow, and I motioned to my mom that I wanted to leave. She gave me "The Eye." There is no need to waste time explaining; you know exactly what I am talking about.

# LIVING PARABLE

After prayer, his wife, who was all of four feet five inches tall, chimed in a few words. Her English was slightly better, and she seemed a little more confident than her husband in communicating. He motioned to her, and she lovingly gave the floor back to him as they went back and forth like a beautiful symphony explaining their work in China.

From smuggling Bibles to supporting underground churches, it was hard to believe that they were part of such incredible work. But before I knew it, I was completely engaged with every word these missionaries were communicating, and I was hoping they would talk for the rest of the night.

The husband began to explain a story that would change my life. He told us about a time that he and his wife were in China. They were going from one place of the city to another and had decided to go in a taxi. He described that while he was sitting in the taxi, the Lord told him to put his Bible to his nose.

As I listened, this sounded "preposterous" to me, even though I had no idea what that word meant at the time. And then, as if replaying the event, he lifted up his Bible and began to place it to his nose. The moment was awkward at best.

His wife took the story from that point.

"I was sitting in the back seat of the taxi next to a man while my husband was sitting in the front seat," she explained. "I thought it was odd that the man did not allow my husband to sit next to me, but my mind was on getting to the next destination, not on the imminent danger before us."

"I obediently sat in the taxi with my Bible to my nose for only a few moments," her husband added. " I asked the Lord, 'Why are You having me hold my Bible to my nose?'"

I could not help but think how ridiculous this must have looked and wondered if this man was crazy. *Was he really hearing from the Lord?*

Then, all of a sudden, the man who was sitting next to his wife revealed a rope in his hand and quickly pulled the rope around the neck of her husband as she watched in fright.

BULLETPROOF BIBLE

The rope caught the Bible, which was resting on her husband's nose, and saved his life. Immediately, the couple was ejected from the moving vehicle into the middle of the street and survived the attack.

I was floored!

*C'mon, this can't be real!* I thought.

The small group that was huddled in our living room was completely silent. I wanted to ask a million questions, but I had been taught that children were to be seen and not heard; so I remained silent. The older Asian couple leaned back with joy while telling the story as if remembering the goodness of the Lord in their lives.

I sat back and made a decision that night. If God could use them, He could use me. I wanted an adventure with Jesus. No longer were my prayers, "Now I lay me down to sleep...."

That night, and every night after that, I prayed to have an adventure with the Lord. In no way, shape or form did I want to sit in a pew and pollute the place with a faith that did not reflect the stories of the Word. For me, the adventure had just begun. The power of this testimony of faithfulness had changed my life forever.

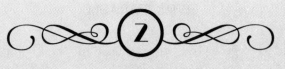

# HIIT
## (HIGH INTENSITY INTERVAL TRAINING)

*"Don't let anyone look down on you because you are young, but set an example for the believers in speech, in conduct, in love, in faith and in purity."—1 Timothy 4:12 (NIV)*

*"God has not given us a spirit of fear, but of power and of love and of a sound mind."—2 Timothy 1:7*

## 1984 - 1985

**"S**wimmers, take your mark...."

My heart was racing and my body felt like a horse behind the gate in the Kentucky Derby. Adrenaline was pumping through my veins, and I was ready to win the race. I was in the center lane, and on either side of me were my rivals from the opposing team. We really didn't like each other, and it made the race all the more important for me to win. I know, it was not the greatest of motives, but God was still working on me.

For several years, I worked hard to get to this place—to be in the finals of the Junior Olympics for my event. I was hoping my time would qualify me for Senior Nationals since my coach would not allow me to go to Junior Nationals. His philosophy was that I should never settle for anything less than the best, and he constantly pushed me to get there. This training would majorly affect my approach to life.

I spent my life in the pool throughout my high school and college years. Morning and evening practices, weekend swim meets, and constant training consumed most of my time. In fact, I remember one of my friends whispering to me in church that I reeked of chlorine and that they were "gagging" from the smell. It was so bad that one Wednesday evening Bible Study, a couple actually moved a few seats away to get a reprieve.

# LIVING PARABLE

I had decided to go all the way and train for the Olympics, which was being held in Seoul, Korea that year. This race would help determine my status for qualifying for the Bahamian team since I was not an American at the time. I put everything I had into training and preparing. I ate right, worked out and did everything my coach told me to do—outside of not going to prom. With so much at stake, I could not believe when I heard the triple beep, I was the one in the water! If you're a swimmer, you know what that means: you are disqualified because you have false started.

The two guys on either side of me had made a plan to move when we were set to swim for the race. That movement heightened my anxiety and caused my body to do what my mind told me not to do—false start! No wonder the Word of God teaches us to take captive our thoughts and have self-control. The ramifications in this case cost me that race and, ultimately, my Olympic dreams.

From that failure, my coach had me practice start after start, after start. There was one practice where I believe we did over 100 starts. Because he was my coach, he recognized a weakness in my race and purposed to put me through proper training to prevent me from repeating that mistake. Some of the things he did, I could not understand. Many of the drills we practiced made no sense to me at all. For example, he would have me start and stop a stopwatch until my reaction time was .02 seconds.

Sure, I get it now. Yet as a teenager, it just made me mad!

I look back on my swimming years and realize that it was more about training than it was swimming. You see, it goes back to the adventure for which I longed. We have a heavenly coach whose name is Jesus. He knows exactly what we need in order to prepare us to win the race that is set before us.

In 1 Corinthians 9, Paul reminds us to run (in my case, swim) in such a way that you win the prize. He tells us to put our bodies into subjection so that we will not be disqualified. This involves training. I have learned that we all like the taste of victory, but very rarely do we like the process of preparing. God knew what I needed in order for me to exceed in the most important event—my life!

# HIIT (HIGH INTENSITY INTERVAL TRAINING)

At thirteen, I discovered an organization willing to send someone my age with a group of young people around the world to share the gospel. More than likely, because of the impact of the Asian missionaries I had met, I chose to go to Korea for three months and help build a church in an area six hours south of Seoul. However, this organization does not simply send you but trains you through a "boot camp" of sorts. And, depending on the nature of your trip, you learn everything from evangelism to carpentry.

For two weeks, we were physically and spiritually challenged. When I heard the alarm go off at 5:30 a.m., and our team had to run an obstacle course before we could eat breakfast, my world came to a collision course with a reality I had not expected. Mission trips were about singing "Kumbaya" and leading people to Christ. What did boot camp have to do with the gospel?

Finally! Our time of commissioning had come, and we were off to Korea. Our journey entailed taking a bus to Los Angeles (LAX) and flying from there to Seoul. This expedition would bring me face to face with another reality I was not prepared for.

Death.

There were two buses that traveled cross-country to LAX. Around Flagstaff, Arizona, our bus was stopped at approximately two o'clock in the morning. A policeman called our leaders off the bus. All we could do was wonder what had happened. The bus was awkwardly silent as we waited for them to let us know what was going on. Upon entering the bus, one of our leaders led us in prayer. His face was somber, and it was obvious that he had recently been crying. Older kids began to whisper, and some of the girls started crying, feeling the tension in the air, without even knowing what had happened. It was after prayer that he began to explain to us that a semi-truck had a head-on collision with the other bus, and two of our leaders and one of the other teammates had been killed instantly.

*How do you handle this at thirteen? How had this happened? Why would God allow His children to suffer in such a manner?* In my mind at that time, it didn't make sense that those going to serve the Lord would encounter such trials and tribulations. You would think there would be supernatural protection for those willing to give their lives for the gospel. Now, I knew the words of Jesus when He said, "In this world you will have tribulation," but at that time nothing made sense at all.

Many people at my home church thought my parents were crazy for allowing me to travel across the world at the age of thirteen. This event could only justify their opinions and quite possibly cause my parents to ask me to come home. Yet, when I talked to them, they provided a peace for me to press on despite the obstacles and serve the Lord at all costs. That counsel would radically affect my worldview and be the basis of many of my decisions in the future.

Upon arrival in Korea, we worked diligently for several weeks to construct a church building in a small village. We lived with the pastor and his family and enjoyed life together as I learned a new culture—daily eating rice, using an outhouse and learning how to build trusses for a roof. The work was hard but rewarding.

Our summer ended in Hong Kong for one week, which was used to debrief our time and prepare us to go home and serve the Lord. This experience allowed us to explore another culture and learn the way of life of another people group. They also took us to China for a day of sightseeing. Yet, this trip would also have a heavenly purpose—our team was chosen to smuggle Bibles into China.

During one of our daily sessions that week, an American missionary who lived in China came to download to our group how we would smuggle the Bibles across the border. I came in late to the meeting, and since there were no more seats available in the small room, I sat on the floor in the back of the building. I'm not sure what happened to me except to say that sleep has no mercy.

Before I knew it, the meeting was over, and the clanging of chairs awakened me as people got up to leave. Everyone was so excited for the following day. So instead of asking what happened in the meeting, I simply acted excited as well, even though I had no idea what we were going to do. The next day, I was handed a bag and told to take it across the border when we got to customs and immigration. I never looked in the bag, nor did I know what I was carrying. When we arrived to cross into China for the day, my whole team looked concerned and was in pockets of prayer preparing for the "big event." I prayed along with them, but it seemed as if even their prayers were in code. I couldn't fully understand the reasons for the prayer and concern. I felt like I was on the TV show, "Mission Impossible" (it wasn't a movie back then) because everyone was so secretive about "the mission" at hand.

I was one of the first to cross without event or mishap. I smiled my way through and "acted" as if nothing was peculiar. The truth be known, I didn't know to be any other way. Supposedly, this gave some courage to my team, and they followed suit allowing our bags to get through. Amazing how God uses us despite us! It was after the crossing that I began to understand what had just happened. My team leader pulled us aside, praised the Lord that our Bibles made it through and began to explain our drop-off points. He reminded us of the process, though it was my first time hearing it, and relayed to us how we would accomplish the task. Now, I was nervous! Thankfully, God blinded me at the perfect time in order to get the job done.

My moment had arrived. I was to take my bag to a fountain and drop it by the edge of the water. After I had completed the mission, I ran hastily to the bus and hurried to the back to gaze out the window to watch the pickup. I didn't know who was going to "risk their life" for the Word, but as soon as I saw him, I knew which one he was. Looking apprehensive and extremely cautious, the young man I suspected walked around the fountain as nonchalantly as he could. Slowly, he walked up to the bag as our bus was driving away from the site. For just a moment, I saw him pick up the Bibles, and his face turned to joy. No longer did he appear worried or concerned; from what I saw, he was completely at peace.

When we returned that evening, I clutched my Bible with a little more sincerity than I ever had. The moment of seeing that young man so blessed to hold the Scriptures in his hand began to shape in me a love for the Word of God like never before. As the psalmist wrote, "Your word is very pure; therefore Your servant loves it" (119:140).

# LIVING PARABLE

I was hooked.

I could not wait to receive the new brochure from this organization, and hoped to travel again the following summer to another country and serve the Lord. Coming from an island only seven by twenty-two square miles, this Bahamian boy was ready to conquer the world for Jesus. At fourteen, I still had a lot of wisdom to gain, but my zeal was ever present.

The Lord led me to pick Liberia, West Africa, as my next destination. We would build a school at a mission compound located in the middle of nowhere. When we landed in Liberia, we had quite a journey ahead of us. That night we traveled about six hours from the capital city to a smaller village on the Cestos River, which we crossed the following day.

As we traveled that night, there were about ten of us in a van that could only seat seven. With our bags on the roof, two Liberian riders and one driver, we scuffled through winding jungle roads in the pitch darkness of night en route to our destination. It was uncomfortable to say the very least. Three other people now occupied my personal space.

About halfway through our trip, we hit an unusual bump and came to a screeching halt. I could not understand the Liberians, but it was apparent that something major had just happened. The van quickly reversed, and we felt the bump again. One of the Liberians jumped out of the vehicle and ran to the front of the van. The next thing we saw was a dancing black man holding the tail of some kind of animal that had the appearance of a large rodent.

The three Liberians rejoiced as if they had just won a million dollars. The one holding the rodent walked to the back, opened the back hatch and threw the animal into the van. For the rest of our trip, all we could hear were the sounds of a dying animal. Oh, and the sounds of our girls getting sick at every whimper of this poor creature as it endured a slow death. We were invited to dinner that evening, and each of us politely asked to be excused.

The next morning, our entire team prepared to cross the river. Expecting to see the Boston whalers and outboards with which I had grown up, I was surprised to see dugout canoes with paddles. Our bodies could barely fit widthwise inside the canoes. Part of the journey involved bailing water; the other part involved calming our girls who were bothered by the plethora of water roaches trying to crawl on them. The river was almost a mile across and the current was very strong in the center, so it took about forty minutes to reach the other side.

The landscape was stunning. Miles of virgin waterway winding through the Liberian countryside, along with the roar of the waves at the river's mouth was absolutely captivating. Water is like a second home for me. However, for one of our leaders from Kansas, who had never seen the ocean before, there was much intrigue but also much concern. Once landed, we still had a seven-mile journey by foot to reach our destination. It would take us about three hours walking since the trail was about the width of a man, and our ceiling was the canopy of tall trees. Several times we came across Liberian driver ants. These nasty little insects have claws they use to cling to you and bite. They travel in hordes. Down the long caravan of people you would hear someone randomly scream, "Ants!" and everyone would take off to avoid getting bit as they ran through their habitat.

Liberia has two seasons—hot and hotter. Unfortunately, we came during the latter, and it seriously felt as if we would melt on the journey. At one point, we had to cross a small river. Even though there was a log crossing above the water, many of us chose to walk right through the river in order to cool off. It was absolutely refreshing since the water was surprisingly cold and clear. We didn't know we were walking through their water supply; all we knew was that we needed to cool down.

Over the years, I have learned many lessons in regards to ministering to others from other countries. Most importantly, ask questions more often than taking action.

The mission was located very close to the beach, so when we were a half hour away, we began to hear the sound of the ocean. The sound of crashing waves hurried our pace, and we wasted no time upon our arrival jumping into the ocean to cool down one more time. Never mind that we were wearing our clothes. The only thing that mattered at that point was getting relief from the heat.

# LIVING PARABLE

The surf that day was amazing. As a surfer, I longed for a board, yet there was something ominous about it being Africa that kept me close to the shore. After a few minutes of playfully being tossed and turned on the beach, I heard a few of our team members screaming at the top of their lungs. James, our leader from Kansas, and three other teammates had gotten caught in a rip current and were being pulled out to sea. Struggling to get back to shore, three of them swam out of the current and worked their way through the rocky shoreline to get back on the beach.

It was at that time we realized that James was not with them. One of our guys, who was a surfer from California, dove into the water to find James. When he returned, he was dragging James' lifeless body; he had drowned before he was able to get to him. For several hours, we performed CPR on James not wanting to believe that he had gone home to be with the Lord. It was as if when James raised his hand for help the last time, the Lord simply grabbed him and brought him home.

I was fourteen. I didn't know how to handle this. In some sense, with the death of my teammates the year before, I began to feel as if I were plagued. *What in the world am I doing living away from my family halfway around the world?* I wondered. I had no idea that serving the Lord was going to be so hard. In theory, I understood when Paul said in Acts 14:22: "We must go through many hardships before we enter the kingdom of God," (NIV) but in practice, who prepares you for such things?

I became a swimmer and a lifeguard upon my return. Out of those ashes, God would begin to make something beautiful. For over seven years, He would form in me self-discipline and the heart to seek and save those who were drowning.

Spiritually, you can connect the dots: As He used sheep to make Moses a shepherd of His people, He used these two trips to cause me to count the cost as I faced the reality of the adventure for which I was asking. This also I understood. Everything in our lives has a purpose. All of our days were written before we came to be. Today, I look back and realize that my life is in His Hands—He is my coach.

# EMPOWERED THROUGH FAITH

*"But none of these things move me; nor do I count my life dear to myself, so that I may finish my race with joy, and the ministry which I received from the Lord Jesus, to testify to the gospel of the grace of God." —Acts 20:24*

## 1986 - 1992

It was completely dark. I could not see my hand in front of my face. I had no idea where I was going but knew that I had to keep walking forward. I could faintly hear the sound of people screaming, so with my hands stretched out in front of me I continued to walk down what seemed to be a hallway.

It was very hot. Though I was not expending a lot of energy, sweat was rolling down my face and my clothes were drenched in perspiration. The darkness seemed evil. There was a tinge of terror with every step I took. In fact, I continued to feel like I needed to run away, but my feet kept moving me toward those horrific screams that kept getting louder and louder.

My hands hit something in front of me. It was a door! I quickly searched for the knob because there appeared to be a light coming from under the crack of the threshold. I desperately wanted out of the darkness no matter what was on the other side; so frantically, I turned the knob and pushed the door to find myself on a ledge that seemed to drop into eternity. The heat was unbearable, and the screams pierced me to the core of my soul like a knife. I looked all around to see how I could help, whom I could help or what I could do to alleviate the ones in pain. All of a sudden, I heard my name.

"Chet!" "Chet, why didn't you tell me?"

I knew that voice. His name was Hyman.

31

# LIVING PARABLE

During my high school years, I knew that God had called me into ministry. I was involved with Campus Life and my home church, yet I also recognized that I had several weaknesses that needed to be strengthened in order for me to pursue this path. One of them, in particular, was my disdain for older people.

At the ripe age of sixteen, I had worked hard, saved my money and bought a 1965 convertible Mustang with my dad. I painted it fire engine red, worked on the engine and replaced the interior. I was ready to show the world how cool I was on the roads of South Florida.

Unfortunately, the roads were littered with "snowbirds." Typically, South Florida's population swells during the winter months when many of the older retirees from up north come down to their winter homes in our area. At that time, I thought that they are not the best drivers; and of course at sixteen I could be the fair judge of their years of experience.

My car was constantly at risk. I know you may be thinking that I am shallow, but keep in mind that I was only sixteen. Consequently, I had developed contempt for the elderly. Our culture doesn't help! We really do not honor older people. Typically, we place them in nursing homes as the only solution, but in some cases it is more a matter of selfish convenience and independence than necessity.

God gave me some insight. If I was going to be used effectively in ministry, I needed to work on my problem. Thus, He led me to volunteer at a nursing home every Tuesday after school for an hour.

To my surprise, I developed incredible relationships with these people. In fact, many of them became close confidants and friends from whom I received much advice. I learned about the Great Depression, World War II, and many wise principles that have guided me throughout my lifetime. We laughed, cried and occasionally caused trouble with the nurses as we found adventure in the halls of the convalescent center.

To the youth, wisdom often appears old and tired; to the aged, zeal often looks young and stupid. However, God was showing me that wisdom and zeal could get married and have great impact! The wet cement of this truth would begin to harden and form in my heart as I spent time with my newfound friends. In fact, it started a lifestyle of seeking seasoned saints to help guide me along life's way.

I'll never forget Agnus. She was a cantankerous old woman who never had anything good to say. I had learned to laugh at her offensive ways, and occasionally she would crack a smile or two. However, I had also learned how far to push. She had been known to throw things, curse profusely or simply say something hurtful until you left her alone. The poor nurses dealt with her every day, but in some strange way had learned to love her antics.

One day, an inspector came to evaluate the nursing home facility. The lady, dressed to the hilt in an ironclad skirt suit, came walking down the hall. She entered the recreation room and ended up talking with Agnus. I simply had to watch this interaction for sheer entertainment.

Question after question, she pummeled Agnus with an inquisition to discover the kind of care she was receiving. At first, Agnus ignored her. I was pleasantly surprised she was not rude or just plain hateful. Agnus had asked the woman to stop asking her questions, but the woman nervously laughed and continued her inquisition. I wanted to laugh but decided to continue my observation.

At one point, I could tell that Agnus had had enough. Her hand was on the table and she was beginning to clench her fist. At first, I thought she was going to punch the lady (she had been known to do that before), but instead, she reached for her fork. Once again, I couldn't believe that she was displaying such self-control, and I had almost turned away thinking that the entertainment was over. Thankfully, I lingered for just a moment longer. In one fell swoop, Agnus, at ninety years old, took the fork and stabbed the lady on the top of her hand. While the fork did not penetrate her skin, the lady yelped in terror.

"I told you to stop asking me questions," Agnus simply said, as she called for the nurse and was wheeled away. You can begin to see why I loved this place! There was one man whom I loved. His name was Hyman. From what I remember, his room was down the first hall to the right after you walked past the dining room in the facility. He was bedridden and did not leave his room too often. Of the hour I spent in the facility, almost thirty minutes was spent with Hyman. Our conversations were always pleasant and informative, and our times together were pretty incredible.

I could tell Hyman everything. He did not judge me, nor did he console me. He would listen and offer his counsel. He was a Jewish man with a rich history in Judaism, and he would often talk about Passover, Israel or the crisis in the Middle East. I would listen and learn about a part of our faith that is not taught in Sunday school, or church that often. Every time I left, I would walk out the door and say, "God bless you, Hyman."

One Tuesday, the Lord spoke to me telling me to share the gospel with him. Not really knowing the voice of the Lord or understanding the sensitivity I needed for the Holy Spirit, I ignored His voice and said to myself that I would tell him next week.

The following Tuesday, I walked into the convalescent center. According to my normal routine, I went into the dining hall to see who was there, greeted the nurses at the nurses' station, took a right turn and went to see Hyman. His room was cleaned and the bed was empty. So I went to the nurses' station.

"Where did you place Hyman?" I asked the nurses.

They looked at each other and with sullen faces looked at me and simultaneously said, "Hyman passed last night."

For a moment, I felt as if someone had punched me in the stomach. All the air in the room had escaped. I was caught in a vacuum, and I needed to breathe.

"Are you all right?" The nurses said in unison. It must have been obvious to them that I was not taking the news too well. Without responding, I walked away, got in my convertible, and drove home.

# EMPOWERED THROUGH FAITH

I tossed and turned in bed that night. Suddenly, I was awakened from my nightmare with Hyman's voice calling my name. My sheets were soaked in sweat. I was thankful to be out of that darkness and no longer hearing those screams. I vividly remember looking down that ledge before I awoke and seeing thousands of people burning in flames. I dropped by my bedside and immediately knew that this dream was something other than a nightmare.

I had a job to do.

There was not a moment to waste.

I must preach the gospel.

I wept bitterly that night. I will never forget the visual of Hyman's face in those flames asking me why I did not tell him the truth. That dream seemed so real and so vivid, yet I knew that it was only a taste of the reality of thousands of people that daily face their eternal destiny.

Truly, hell was created for Lucifer and his angels, but God sent His Son that we might have everlasting life. I learned that I am His ambassador and His minister of reconciliation. God was making His man!

When I entered college, I developed a fervency to be in ministry. I knew I had to get onto the mission field, and my desire was to return to the shores of Liberia. I was sure that I was going to be a doctor; so I majored in biology, took the MCAT and applied to ten universities. My dream schools were the University of Southern California or the University of North Carolina at Chapel Hill. All four of my years in college were geared toward attending either of them and then, off to medical missions.

As God would have it, I got denied at all ten of the schools at which I applied. Devastated, I went back to the Lord and questioned His direction for my life. Instead of running a personal inventory of my own ambitions and direction, I immediately concluded that He was the problem. Like Martha, I went to Him in prayer feeling like I was doing the right thing and He had done the wrong thing.

As gently as He did with Martha in Luke 10, that still, small voice began to speak that my direction was not His direction for my life.

# LIVING PARABLE

"Are you willing to lay it all down and follow Me," He asked.

"You are talking about laying down my dreams!" I replied.

This was my ambition. I wanted to make my father proud, and to have a doctor in the family would be his pride and joy. I had worked so hard in high school and college to become a physician, and after all of that, Jesus wanted me to lay it down. Even the thought of it still makes me sweat today. I did not realize that I could not present my plan to Him expecting His blessing; I had to go to Him for His plan for me and receive it.

As difficult as it was, Jesus really did not leave me with any other options. He only gave me one choice—I figured even the University of Guam would not accept me. At that point, I knew I was to graduate and go to Liberia. That semester I took twenty-six credit hours in order to finish college and get to the mission field. I had been accepted by a foreign mission board to teach at one of their schools in Liberia, and they wanted me to be there in August.

I had to take a teacher's exam to be an instructor at the school in Liberia. I had not taken one education course, so I bought a test prep book and began to go through it in order to prepare for the exam. I couldn't understand anything and decided that if this were Jesus' plan for my life, He would need to give me supernatural knowledge to pass. In essence, I was trying to set the Lord up for failure. Crazy, I know, but I really wanted to be a doctor.

On the Saturday morning of the test, I remember driving to the university and talking with the Lord. I prayed, "Father, You know that I desire to be a doctor. It seems that You have taken this opportunity from me in order to do with me as You please. I know that You always have a good, pleasing and perfect plan for my life. Please help me to embrace Your plan and empower me to pass this test."

For four hours, I sat taking the test. Truly, I made a 'guesstimated' answer on almost every question. I walked out thinking that it would be a miracle if I succeeded. Sure enough, miracle granted! Two weeks later, I discovered that I had passed. The road was undeniable. I was on my way to Liberia as a teacher. Ugh! Almost as a foreshadowing of my coming experience in Liberia, I had planned to leave the week that Hurricane Andrew hit South Florida. I was faced with a decision to get out early or possibly be delayed for several weeks since the reports were saying that Andrew had the potential to cause a lot of damage.

Through prayer, I decided to head out and fly to New Jersey, where I would meet up with other missionaries who were on their way to Liberia as well. Because I was leaving early, I connected with some missionary friends that lived in New Jersey and thought it would be good to stay with them, as they had served in Liberia for many years.

While there, Hurricane Andrew hit South Florida. Its tempestuous winds and tornados destroyed most everything that was in its path. The pictures on the news were unbelievable. There was cataclysmic devastation as people were without homes, water and electricity. As well, I discovered that my stay in New Jersey would be longer since Liberia had an uprising of rebel activity within the country, and our field supervisor delayed our trip.

I was bummed!

*I should have stayed home*, I thought to myself. Yet, I really had sensed that the Lord wanted me to leave early. He had confirmed it in Scripture and with godly counsel.

For two weeks, I sat in New Jersey wondering, *What am I doing here?* I could not fly back because the airport was closed. To be honest, for ten of the fourteen days I did nothing but mope.

"Please, speak to me," I cried to the Lord one morning. On my knees, beside the bed with the Scriptures opened, I waited in silence for Him to speak. It seemed as if I had been there for about an hour; however, it may have been more than that because I think I fell asleep. All right, I fell asleep!

Around mid-morning, I was awakened. Suddenly, I felt like I was not the only person in the room. The man I was staying with was not at home, and the presence seemed extraordinary. I didn't look up for the moment was holy. The room was transformed into a sanctuary, and I sensed the warmth and comfort of the Holy Spirit. I began to sing songs of worship, but suddenly silence overtook me.

The Lord was there.

His presence seemed so physical and tangible that I bowed prostrate on the floor and reached one of my hands up, as if pleading for amnesty in the presence of the King. It was at that moment I experienced the touch (anointing) of the Holy Spirit.

While it was gloriously supernatural, it also felt very normal, and my body did not shake or tremble as we have seen on Christian television. All I could sense was His love and power coming over me, and it reminded me of how a father would hold his child who was simply in need of strength and security.

I laid there for several minutes in awe of this moment. Tears flowed down my face as I realized that in the busyness of my departure, I had forgotten to pack one thing—the power of the Holy Spirit. Grateful that He would not allow me to leave until I was spiritually prepared, I began to praise and worship Him for the power from on high.

I had no idea what was before me, but now I know who was with me. As Paul said, "And see, now I go bound in the Spirit to Jerusalem (Liberia), not knowing the things that will happen to me there, except that the Holy Spirit testifies in every city, saying that chains and tribulations await me. But none of these things move me; nor do I count my life dear to myself, so that I may finish my race with joy, and the ministry which I received from the Lord Jesus, to testify to the gospel of the grace of God" (Acts 20:22-24).

Purposed to tell the gospel and empowered from on high, I was ready to be sent out for the work for which Jesus had prepared me. In some sense, I wish I had taken greater notice of the storm I watched on TV, as God was using it to forewarn me of the coming trial. Yet, it is probably best I didn't; for had I known, I may have turned around in New Jersey and not fulfilled the ministry that was given to me for His glory.

# VICTORIOUS FAILURE

*"Not that I have already attained, or am already perfected; but I press on, that I may lay hold of that for which Christ Jesus has also laid hold of me."— Philippians 3:12*

*"You are of God, little children, and have overcome them, because He who is in you is greater than he who is in the world."—1 John 4:4*

## 1992

I t was 2 a.m. and I was awakened from sleep—a usual occurrence in Liberia. I heard *"Cccccchhhhhheeeeeetttt"* buzzing in my ear. The mosquitos had come to know me personally. The relentless heat and humidity through the night often caused me to take bucket showers with tepid water and sleep on the tile.

The constant threat of someone breaking in magnified every noise and movement through the night to the point that I felt like a hunted deer whose hearing remained alert and sense of smell sharpened for survival. Indubitably, sleep was a precious commodity when it came and having it disturbed was to wake from your dreams into a nightmare.

However, this disturbance was different from what I had heard before. It was neither the familiar sound of soldiers marching on the road to ensure curfew, nor the crows of a rooster informing us all that morning was in short order. This sound was more like the hissing of a snake, so I quickly found my flashlight that was always by my head and began to look around.

I hate snakes with a passion. I am almost convinced that God hates them as well. I often wondered why God would send me to the one country in Africa where the most prevalent creatures are deadly snakes! Be that as it may, I found none slithering as I searched the floor in my room, yet this sound had gotten louder.

# LIVING PARABLE

I looked out of my window. The sky was lit up with a streak of fire shooting through the darkness of the night. At first, I thought a comet was passing since it was too large to simply be a falling star. Surely, I would have heard if this were the case, so my mind began to wonder for a few moments as to what this could be. Without much time to think, the streak passed out of sight. Then I saw a light that mushroomed in the darkness, heard a sound, felt a rumble, and immediately I knew what was going on.

We had been attacked.

Since I had arrived in Liberia, there had been threats of attacks from the rebel forces that controlled most of the country outside the capital city of Monrovia. We had listened to the threatening rants from their leader, Charles Taylor, but I had paid no attention to his foolish tirades because they seemed so bombastically preposterous. Besides, though war was a reality to Liberians, it was only a movie to me. In other words, because I had never experienced the toils of war, I had no context other than the war flicks I had seen in the comfort of the United States of America.

I had been intrinsically deceived.

A few minutes after the bomb had landed and exploded, I could hear the sound of gunfire. It seemed as if it was only a block away because of the artillery being used. In reality, the front was about five miles from where we were staying. Missionary and Liberian alike who were living in the community came outside and broke curfew to hear and see what was happening. Liberians looked dreadfully afraid while the missionaries appeared to be trying to keep it together. I think the Liberians knew exactly what was ahead, and the missionaries simply had no idea.

Ignorance is bliss.

I could say quite confidently that my ignorance shone like the noonday sun. While I had grown accustomed to curfew and rumors of war, I truly had not taken any of this seriously because it was so far out of my realm of understanding.

Like this one evening after curfew when I wanted to take a bucket bath. I had been lazy that day to fill my barrel in the bathroom with water, so I decided to go down to the well, fill my bucket, shower by the well and return home happily. First, you must understand that we had no running water. Every day, in order to have household water, you had to walk down a hill, fill your buckets from the well, walk back up the hill, empty your buckets in a barrel and repeat the process again. (My leg muscles have never been as strong as they were at the end of that year.)

*Who wanted to do that every day?*

Not me!

Quietly, I opened my door, found the path to the well and carefully followed it by the light of the moon. Lowering my bucket, I was able to fill it with water and placed it beside the well. I took off my clothes, slapped some water on me and began to lather up to bathe. About the time I had finished getting most of the soap off of me, I heard footsteps down by the road. It was the usual march of the peacekeeping soldiers that ensured our curfew. I crouched down in the tall grass hoping that they did not see or hear me.

One of them fired their M-16. I was in shock.

Was that a warning?

Was it a coincidence?

They could not have been firing at me—or could they? In any case, my body took off without any conscious effort on my part to consider a plan. As I ran up the hill, another shot went off. I had no clothes on; the moon was shining, and I was glowing like Casper the ghost but running as fast as Flash Gordon!

The missionary house next to my home hosted two older women who were in their seventies. They had each served the Lord in Liberia for over thirty years. As I was blazing a trail across the mission compound, I could hear one of them shout out the window, "Chet, is that you?"

Humiliated, I didn't respond and ran to my room, and I never disregarded curfew again. No one brought it up the following day, so the mystery remained as to what that "thing" was that darted across the grass that night. In spite of my understanding, war was upon us. In the days that followed, our field director had planned to send all the missionaries to Ivory Coast. I did not want to leave and discussed my opinion with Glenn.

# LIVING PARABLE

Glenn was an African-American about thirty-five years old at the time who walked with Jesus intimately. Confident and secure as a leader, he is an incredible man who discipled me throughout my stay in Liberia. I am so grateful for the way he handled my plea that day; he took it to the Lord in prayer.

In my heart, I believed that this war had not caught God off guard. My parents had raised me to trust Him in all things, and now this calling was being put to the test. You see, if the Lord is omniscient to foresee the future, and had indeed sent me to Liberia; then, in my mind, He sent me to be there during this crisis. That logic made sense to me. After much prayer, Glenn allowed me to stay and sent the rest of the missionaries to Ivory Coast.

For the next several months, the war raged around us. We consistently saw fighter planes fly over us. The Liberians called them "du-du" birds because they dropped their "mess," and nobody was there to clean it up. Rebels would try to break the bufferzone barriers and one time actually succeeded. In fact, I'll never forget the day this happened.

An older Liberian woman was cooking me a special Liberian dish called "fufu." It is a starchy, gelatinous white ball of fermented cassava. I know it sounds interesting, but for me, it was much better than eating rice every day. In any case, as I ran home, I saw her running out of my house with all of my things on her head.

"Where are you going?" I asked her.

"Out of here!" She exclaimed, as she ran out the door. The amazing thing was that she had saved my things by wrapping them in a bed sheet and placing them on her head, willing to leave her own things behind. I learned a lot that day.

Panic filled the hearts of the Liberians as schools were closed and businesses shut down. Life became absorbed with listening to BBC every day and wondering when we would have to run. In order not to go crazy, I hosted volleyball and soccer tournaments. With sounds of gunfire in the background and jets flying above, you could hear through the chaos, "Four serving five!"

# VICTORIOUS FAILURE

It's amazing what you can adapt to, but hey, it brought peace to our hearts. The church organized a series of spiritual events. I had never participated in a corporate fast and prayer, but in these times, everyone was crying out to God for His supernatural intervention. They had determined to do a three-day fast. This was foreign to me. I had given up breakfast or lunch before, but never a whole day. In my twenty-two years, God was infusing the power of prayer into my life in a way that I had never experienced before.

Day one had passed, and I thought I would die. Day two almost killed me. I spent day three shopping in town as if I was planning for three families to join us for a Thanksgiving meal. I'm sorry to admit that this fast brought me to God in prayer more to survive those three days than for any other thing! I have grown since then.

Finally, six o'clock arrived—the time we decided to break the fast. We spent most of the day cooking over an open fire, baking in a unique, coal-fired oven made from an old refrigerator and prepping the table to sit and eat. Our plan was to celebrate the end of the fast by turning the generator on and watching one of the Christian classics that we had on hand.

The truth is I ate like a pig! I ate like there was no tomorrow. I ate until it hurt to move. I was ashamed of myself, but I could not stop. Looking back, it is pitiful to think how I made something so spiritual so carnal. I realize now how gracious our God is to protect us for His glory alone. Praise be to God!

After the meal we settled down to watch a movie. We turned the generator on and it was incredible to see electricity. We had not used the generator for months, as we were concerned that rebels would hear it and attack the mission to steal it. Things had seemed to settle, relatively speaking, so we took the risk.

About thirty minutes into the movie, my stomach began to rumble. I was very uncomfortable and started to get that infamous feeling of "get to the bathroom quickly." I politely excused myself from the room, walked outside while my stomach was cramping and began to go up the trail toward my home.

# LIVING PARABLE

I had reached the one and only streetlight on the whole mission compound when I heard a familiar voice call out my name.

"Hey, Chet!"

It was Tiepo. He was a good friend of mine and wanted to talk. He was an unusually tall Liberian man, as most Liberians are around five feet eight to ten inches tall.

I could hear my bathroom calling my name and my stomach in agreement, so I tried to continue walking forward as he was running toward me. It did not work. He caught me under the streetlight and wanted to share something with me that was very important to him at the time.

I figured it would take just a moment, but the story went on for a little bit longer than what my stomach could afford. I did not want to interrupt him but knew I needed to go. In desperation, I decided to release some air, hoping it would relieve me of the painful spasms that were turning my insides upside down. Unfortunately, I did not realize it was like the cap of a shaken Coke bottle that when opened, there is no stopping the explosion.

I desperately tried to hold things together, but the magnitude of what I had eaten earlier was simply paying me back in humiliation for the trauma to which I had subjected my internal organs.

I looked at Tiepo and said, "I need to go!"

Under the one and only streetlight that illuminated my being, he looked at me and said, "I think you already did."

Mortified, I ran toward my house. Unfortunately, the retribution of my stomach had fallen onto my flip-flops, and I slipped midway through my trot landing on my posterior. I had completely lost all dignity at that point. Note to self: Do not eat a lot after a long fast; your body will pay you back!

The war also caused mosquitos to go awry. People were no longer concerned with standing water, and the government was no longer spraying the roads to combat these deadly insects. Oftentimes, when you walked into your house at night, their buzzing was as loud as an alarm without the snooze button! Getting malaria was inevitable, and my turn had come.

# VICTORIOUS FAILURE

Malaria is the world's number one killing disease. The impact of this malady in Sub-Saharan Africa had caused the death of millions of people. Various prophylaxes can be taken to avoid getting the disease, but with the war and limited medications, many people were getting sick on a regular basis.

The best way to describe malaria is that it makes you feel like you are baking in an oven at about 450 degrees. Much like a severe flu, with malaria your joints get stiff, a migraine comes upon you and you'd rather die than get the fever one more time. The fever comes every twenty-four hours or so. Your body is reacting to the breakdown of red blood cells as this little "beastie" is multiplying within you. It is a difficult experience; all you want to do is lie down, hoping to make it through.

Food was also in short supply. Therefore, we decided to purchase 100-pound bags of rice from a local Lebanese merchant. We distributed these bags to the teachers of the school at which I taught. In this way, their families could eat since there was no income from the school to pay salaries.

We distributed the rice at my house where it had been dropped for safe storage. That day, I was recovering from a bad bout of malaria, so when the teachers showed up, I stayed in my room while the administrators of the school dispersed the bags. One by one, the teachers took their bags of rice and went home rejoicing.

I was miserable. My fever had just broken, and the only thing I could do was lie there and try to gain some strength. As I did, I heard a woman faintly crying outside my window. Everyone had left, and she was unable to carry her bag of rice to the road. I sat in my room and listened to her whimper, praying that someone would come and help her. Thirty minutes passed, and no one had come.

About that time, the Lord began to impress upon my heart to carry the bag of rice for her. Immediately, I indignantly responded that there was no way I had the strength or desire to do any such thing! With faithful persistence, God would not leave me alone. I wrestled with Him in prayer on that bed, dictating that this impression could not be from Him since He was a loving God and knew my condition. Besides, she didn't even know I was in the room. Of course, *He* won. I got out of bed, but I had the worst attitude you could imagine. I marched to the door, slammed it shut, walked outside and said, "I'll carry your bag," with my teeth clenched.

Mary, the teacher, was overwhelmed with joy because it was getting late and transportation was going to be rough. I don't think I said a word. The whole way to the road, I carried the bag of rice on my head like the Liberians did. She praised the Lord with every step we took, singing and making melody in her heart to Jesus for sending me.

I was mad.

Her song sounded like a clanging symbol.

Not only was I upset with God for making me do this, but I was also upset with myself for not participating in her praise.

We got to the road, and I threw the bag of rice onto the pavement. She literally jumped with joy and thanked me profusely as I walked away to the sounds of her continuing praise to Jesus. As I walked up the hill back to my house, I couldn't hold my anger anymore and quipped, "Why did You do this to me?" No need to explain to whom I was referring.

It just made no sense to me at all.

After recovering from malaria, I decided to continue a discipleship group that I had begun with twelve young men. I had selected students from my classroom who were either in the tenth or eleventh grade. Because of the war, many of their academic pursuits had been postponed and delayed. Therefore, though they were in the tenth grade, they were between nineteen to twenty-two years of age. As I was twenty-two at the time, it made for great camaraderie and accountability.

One of the young men was very hesitant to join the group. In fact, he really did not want to participate. That surprised me since all of the others were very enthusiastic about being discipled. It seemed that he enjoyed my class but never really wanted to get close enough to have a conversation unless it involved having a discussion about something he did not understand in the lesson. Surprisingly, one day he came up to me and wanted to join the group. I was thrilled. I really thought that this young man had a lot of potential, and I wanted to invest into him, even though we were about the same age. We spent the next nine months of my yearlong stay becoming great friends and growing in Christ together. At the end of my term, these young men hosted an event to celebrate all that God had done in our lives together. We had truly grown in relationship with each other but most importantly, with the Lord.

The discipleship went both ways, as it always should, and we recognized the goodness of God to further conform us into the image of His Son, Jesus Christ. Each one gave a testimony of God's grace that evening. It truly was a special night. Even though there was war, famine and disease, these holy men decided to rejoice in how God had used their trial to make them more like Jesus.

When Daniel, the one who was resistant to relationship, spoke, he started by saying that he did not want to be a part of the group. Daniel was an honest young man who spoke his mind. His laugh always made me smile. It was so unique; his whole being seemed to enjoy the moment, and you could not help but start laughing as well—whether the joke was funny or not.

Daniel went on to say that something happened that changed his mind. One day, as he was cleaning the school in fulfillment of his work scholarship, he looked out the window and saw me carrying the bag of rice for the teacher. Immediately, my joy was turned to sorrow; for I could only imagine, with my attitude that day, what he was about to say.

"I had never seen a white man help a black woman in that manner and realized that something was different about you," he said. "Your faith seemed genuine, and I wanted to learn how to become that person."

Once again, I was humbled. God had answered my prayer asking why He had me carry the bag. I was embarrassed for my behavior toward the Lord and went to my room that evening and repented. I thought of Stephen and how he had the face of an angel when he was being stoned and went so far as to ask the Father to forgive those that were stoning him. I thought of how his sacrifice would change the face of Christianity by revealing to the apostle Paul the overwhelming measure of God's goodness and grace. I compared Stephen's approach to my own and realized that I had a long way to go in order to be like Christ. Truly, in my weakness, He was strong.

I am grateful for the grace of God to allow me to stay in the context of war that year in Liberia. Through the reality of the conflict that physically surrounded me, I began to see the war that I fight within me each and every day.

It is real, and it is powerful, but we have the victory because of Jesus. He is faithful despite our faithlessness because He cannot deny Himself. It is His power that works in us mightily. Therefore, we press on though we may lose some battles because greater is He that is in us than he that is in the world.

## 5

# BLACK COBRAS AND JUJU

*"For we do not wrestle against flesh and blood, but against principalities, against powers, against the rulers of the darkness of this age, against spiritual hosts of wickedness in the heavenly places."—Ephesians 6:12*

## 1993

Liberians are famous for the sayings of the 'old people.' "Hurry, hurry bust trouser" is indicative of the fact that if you rush around to get something done, you will eventually split your pants. Another is, "If you mind the noise in the market, you won't buy good fish," which carefully explains that if you listen to everyone instead of making your own decisions, you may miss out on a great opportunity.

"When at peace, prepare for war" is my favorite saying because it describes the lifestyle of a believer and pretty much sums up the letter to the Ephesians. Paul reminds us, "For we do not wrestle against flesh and blood but against principalities...against the rulers of darkness of this age."

In our modern world of technology, it seems that the enemy attacks us shrewdly through our music, movies and more. However, we must remember that he is an angel of light, and we cannot be ignorant of his devices. Lies, deceit, fear and doubt are at the vociferous root of his strategies, but they can come at us either subtly or directly. Our enemy will use whatever tactic is necessary to kill, steal and destroy.

Thus, it is vital to remember, "When at peace, prepare for war." With this concept in mind, my pastor's wife had told me during my preparation for leaving for Liberia as a single man to write down all of the promises the Lord gave me in His Word. In that way, I could refer back to my journal during the hard times and remember that the goodness of the Lord was what brought me to Liberia and would sustain me each step of the way.

Little did I know that she was preparing me for war by having me take up the sword of the Spirit, which is the Word of God. Andrea and I had been in the crux of our relationship before I left. She knew I was called to Liberia, but neither of us had counted the cost of what it would mean to be separated for a year. By leaving her, I knew there was a risk that she would find someone else, but I had to trust the Lord for her life as well as my own.

My parents thought I was making a terrible mistake by choosing to leave as they thought I would never find anyone else willing to marry me and go to Liberia. They were right. I would not find anyone, but God would find that someone. I was learning to depend on Him.

During the year I was gone, my mom decided to take Andrea into our home as her maid "of sorts." She would come and clean the house only to enter into conversations that would build their relationship and also train my soon-to-be-wife in the ways of the "Lowe men."

I thank God for that year because it strengthened Andrea's faith and built a lifelong relationship between her and my mom that would get us through many trials. The two of them became like Ruth and Naomi. In some sense this is good, but on the other hand, husbands beware!

The hardest times to be away were the holidays. In fact, Christmas that year was very lonely. Since all the other missionaries were gone, I felt somewhat alone even though friends who had become family over the course of the civil crisis surrounded me. We all depended on each other in various ways; but that year there was no tree, no turkey, no family and no hint of the weather cooling down to give some semblance of what I knew to be the Christmas holiday.

I went to bed Christmas Eve thankful that I had stayed, yet wondered what the other missionaries were doing in the Ivory Coast where they had sought refuge while war waged in Liberia. During that time, I learned what it meant to be Liberian. As there were no other Americans around, I was forced to pick up the dialect, eat only Liberian food and listen for hours to people telling their stories of the previous war. It was fascinating.

Food was scarce for Christmas. Meat was scarcer. Even the meat that was available had obviously sat out in the hot, open-air market for hours, quite possibly for several days. You would have to boil it for hours before considering eating it. The taste had somewhat of a tang, but according to 1 Timothy 4:5, "Everything is sanctified by the Word of God and prayer."

I clung to this Scripture as I walked through the market and watched women swish hundreds of flies off the meat as I passed by.

I also had to get used to different kinds of meat. Pigs' feet and chicken feet are quite the delicacy though different than the ham and turkey I was used to. Sincerely, I learned to love them. However, there were some things that were rather difficult for me to swallow. In fact, I will never forget a time when I was invited to a friend's house to eat.

On our way there, I asked, "What's for dinner?"

She and her husband bent down, picked up a weed and said, "This." I laughed, thinking they were joking, but quickly realized they were not. Upon arriving at their home for dinner that evening, they served the rice and then brought out the covered dish that held the traditional soup containing the meat. Liberians will often mix and match all kinds of meat to flavor their soups, from fish to pigs' feet.

As I expected, every meat you could imagine was inside the delectable dish. However, I was not prepared for what happened next. Happily, the wife came out of the kitchen so thankful for what they had caught that day. The way she talked about it made me think they had killed a chicken or found some deer (I love venison).

The wife walked toward me with the dish and opened the top. She scooped an iguana out of the bowl and placed it on my rice. All I could think of were the words of Jesus to eat whatever is put before you. How I wished that particular verse had not been included in the Scriptures at that moment. Just as I was thinking how I would stomach this smoked creature lying dead on my plate, the husband said, "Wait till you see what's inside!"

# LIVING PARABLE

He quickly cut the belly of the lizard and out flowed her eggs over my plate. He grabbed one before it rolled onto the floor and popped it into his mouth. I thought I would vomit. Truly, I was not at home for Christmas that year. The Christmas goose had been replaced by smoked iguana.

Christmas had the potential to be like any other morning in Liberia. Roosters would crow before the sun would rise. Various households would be in worship and prayer for their morning devotions. Women and children would begin the clanging of pots and pans as they cleaned what had been used the night before. Children would be making noise at the well, arguing over who got there first and who should be able to pump their water next. Men would be either gathering tools for the farm or yelling at their kids to do morning chores. With all of those sounds at one time, it had almost become a symphony that could lull you to sleep once you had gotten used to it.

But Christmas morning was unusually quiet. In fact, it was the silence that awakened me as I had come to enjoy the various sounds of community within my newfound culture. I found it somewhat eerie that the only thing I could hear was the sound of a rooster crowing in the faint distance. It was early; so I figured that since it was Christmas morning, everyone was taking a break from their usual routine, drifting in and out of REM and enjoying the coolness of the morning breeze. That moment was short-lived.

*Pow!*

I had also grown accustomed to the sound of M-16s and AK-47s. In fact, I had gotten to the place of knowing the sounds of different artillery in order to note which faction was closest. This sound, however, was way too close.

*Pow! Pow!*

There was no mistake, it sounded like the front was only fifty to a hundred yards away. *Pow!*

A bullet hit my building, and I immediately was on the floor underneath the window. It is amazing how, when you have no idea what to do, somehow you do the right thing.

# BLACK COBRAS AND JUJU

*Pow! Pow!*

I couldn't believe it.

We were under attack.

On Christmas!

I began to pray, "O Lord, what am I doing here?" You would think I would have sought the Lord for His divine protection, but out of the abundance of the heart the mouth speaks. Jesus does not lie!

My heart was bent on survival and my lips were busy proclaiming it. When the gunfire began to settle, for some reason I thought of my journal. I know now that the Lord was speaking to me, but at the time, I was somewhat surprised that this was the first thing that came to mind. I army-crawled on the floor to the other side of my bed because bullets were still flying. I opened the cabinet and pulled out my journal. Opening it to the first page, I began to read all of the promises the Lord had spoken to me:

"Have I not commanded you? Be strong and of good courage; do not be afraid, nor be dismayed, for the Lord your God is with you wherever you go" (Joshua 1:9).

"Fear not, for I am with you; be not dismayed, for I am your God. I will strengthen you, yes, I will help you, I will uphold you with My righteous right hand" (Isaiah 41:10).

As I read these Scriptures, the Lord began to truly strengthen me with His Word. Though the gunfire did not stop immediately, I was settled in my heart. There was nothing I could do to protect myself. I had to get to the place of trusting in the Lord and choosing to lean not on my own understanding.

Through the morning, this was a process as doubt and fear would set in, but because I had prepared for war with the Word, Jesus brought me back to the place of peace. I was forever grateful for my pastor's wife who knew exactly what I would need in the midst of battle—the Word of God.

Eventually, the gunfire came to a halt. It was relieving to discover that it was simply a group of drunken soldiers celebrating the Christmas holiday. They were not glorifying Jesus on this day of celebrating His birth, but He surely used them in my life to bring me to the Word.

This is why Joseph was able to say, "What you meant for evil, God meant for good," when he was talking to his brothers in Genesis 50. If you were to sum up the amount of good things and bad things that happen in our lives, I guarantee they would almost equal each other. The truth is, positive and negative experiences are a part of life. The greater truth is that though the enemy purposes to hurt us, we can trust that "all things work together for good to those who love God and are called according to His purpose" (Romans 8:28).

Remember, the Word is not our only weapon in this spiritual war that constantly rages around us. We also have prayer and fasting. Keep in mind the sayings of the old people, "When at peace, prepare for war." We cannot expect to go into battle without training.

In the same way, a professional football player cannot expect to perform well if he has not practiced all season. The disciples learned this lesson when they were not able to cast out the demon from a young boy because they lacked the spiritual disciplines of fasting and prayer. Jesus made it clear to them that they had little faith. I had to learn this lesson in a similar way.

As you probably know, the enemy will use direct or subtle attacks to cause havoc in our lives. In Liberia, the people believe in, and some even worship, the demonic. There are many satanic practices. In fact, the root of Haitian voodoo is found on the west coast of Africa through the ancient "juju" practices of the Liberians. To this day, powders, potions and spells remain within the context of their societies. Sadly, these practices have also worked their way into the church, and oftentimes, you will hear the fear in Christians' voices as they talk about their real experiences.

When I was growing up as a child, I thought this type of demonic activity was only found in incredible Bible stories. For me, the Devil had become a caricature of a little red man, holding a pitchfork and smiling deviously like a bad little boy.

This image, promoted by various cartoons I watched growing up as a child, was the perfect delusion to prevent me from seeing things in a spiritual context. However, the Lord would open my eyes to the reality of this spiritual world in a way for which I was not prepared—war.

There was a small village at the bottom of the hill by the community in which I lived. It was located right on the seashore, and most of the men that lived in the settlement were fishermen. There was a tall cotton tree that stood as a skyscraper over the town. Many people rumored that this tree had a "witch." When a Liberian used this term, the indication was that it was satanically used for dark purposes. In Liberia's history, these tall trees would be used to mark villages in the jungle so that lost sojourners could find their way back home.

It was a very poor village, and residents would often make their way to my home to ask for food, money or any type of daily need. Usually, I would not give all of what was requested but would find something to give them in order to build relationship.

Through this, I was able to make friends with the chief of the village. He was a short, stocky fellow. Like most of the fishermen in Liberia, he had a large torso due to hauling nets filled with fish. Though he was the chief, he always dressed like a pauper and never seemed to be pretentious or hold his position higher than his responsibility. I enjoyed our visits.

One day, he came to me and asked me, "Chet, would you follow me to my home?" His daughter was not well, and he wanted me to pray for her.

"I think she is demon possessed," he explained as we walked from my house down the short path to his home.

I laughed, thinking that he was wonderfully simple and began to ask questions about her various symptoms, as if I could come up with some kind of medical answer to solve her problems.

His home was hot.

There was a very low ceiling, and I could hardly stand upright inside. The aroma of smoked fish filled the home. It was so strong that it was as if they had a plug-in with that scent releasing the odor. The whole family gathered in the large room when I arrived. His daughter came out of a room and sat on the floor beside me. He began to re-explain her various symptoms, and I began to think of getting her some Cipro. For me, it was the antibiotic of choice; it seemed to cure anything. Quite frankly, I would take one every other week just to be sure to kill anything in my body that should not be there. (Kids, don't try that at home.)

"Please, pray for her," the chief repeated.

*Well, of course, I'll pray for her,* I thought. You would think this would be the first thing I would think of, especially because of a recent experience. Unfortunately, I, the missionary, had to be reminded to move from the material to the spiritual by a clan chief who was looking to me to provide some spiritual guidance.

I laid my hands on the girl to pray for her. She shivered under my hand and looked at me very strangely. In fact, she looked at me with evil intent. At that moment, I could feel a sense of fear come over me. She got off the ground and stared at me as I was sitting down. She was trying to intimidate me, and honestly, there was something about her way that was succeeding.

I thought back to her dad telling me how he thought she was demon possessed, so I said to her, "Say Jesus is Lord."

I think I had seen that in some movie or something, and I knew in Scripture that only believers could say this. I was abysmally ashamed that I had not considered this possibility more seriously. Knowing my weakness, she looked at me and began to speak in a deeper voice. It was not her voice.

My eyes bugged out of my head. I remembered the story in Acts in which the seven sons of Sceva were tossed around by a demon, and I did not want to get entangled in such a brawl. So, I did the best thing I could think of—I left.

As I was walking briskly out of the house, her father asked me, "Where are you going?"

"This requires much prayer and fasting," I said, and I did not turn around the entire way home. I felt defeated, yet I came to a point in my walk where I realized I needed an empowering upgrade of my faith that could only come with much prayer and fasting. The next day, as I was walking home from the market to my house, I was still contemplating the event from the day before. How could I be on the mission field and not have been prepared?

My mind raced with what I could have or should have done, but the truth was—I had abandoned my post. Almost home, I looked over to the side of the path and noticed a long, cylindrical log. It was very black and caught my attention; I had not seen it there before. It seemed to shimmer in the sunlight, and I could not help but stare at it. Then, it moved. I thought my eyes were playing a trick on me, but it moved again.

This was no stick.

It was a cobra, and it was slithering its way in a perpendicular path that would intersect my direction several feet in front of me. I yelled at the top of my voice, "Snake!"

I knew that Liberians love to kill snakes, and for some reason, my instinct was to get others involved in eradicating this creature that was even cursed by God. A few men, as well as some young boys, joined me and together we saw the snake move quickly on a direct path to my house. It found its way into the bushes, and as if it was on a mission, purposely tried to get into the window.

The weight of the snake moved the entire hibiscus tree, but when it hit the screen and bounced off, the snake fell to the ground and slithered toward my front door. It went up the steps and tried to get through the entrance. Thankfully, the screen door prevented its intrusion and the snake turned to fight.

The black cobra frantically came down the front steps and coiled itself into position to lift up its head, fan out its neck and begin spitting venomous poison in our direction. The men and the boys hurled rocks in its direction until one young boy threw a frontal hit dead on, and the snake went down immediately. One of the men dropped a large rock on its head and the snake's nervous system gave one last jolt throughout its body and died.

# LIVING PARABLE

The same man quickly cut off its head, as I imagine David did with Goliath on the field that faithful day. Now that it was dead, I bravely picked up the snake with a stick and took a picture of it. The cobra was about ten feet long and after we took pictures, we burned the snake in the field as if to ensure that it was truly dead.

That evening, a little boy came from the village below and asked us if we had heard about the witch woman in the town who had died. He explained that she had suddenly passed and that her house had burned down. It was hard to believe, and I did not go back down to verify, but the Liberians made it very clear that she had sent the snake and had to die with it. This experience opened my eyes to the reality of our warfare.

This snake seemed to have a purpose in mind to get into my home. That visual has been a constant reminder to me that our enemy is still the serpent of old. He is packed with venom and ready to strike, deceitfully lying like a snake in the grass wanting to destroy our faith. I have learned that if I want to be a man of faith, I must put into practice disciplines of faith so that when the enemy attacks unawares, I am prepared. Having the Word to guide us, prayer to sustain us and fasting to discipline us, we can be prepared for war at all times.

Maybe each of us needs to put this into practice, "When at peace, prepare for war!" In this, I know I need to be a man of the Word, purposed in prayer and diligent in fasting.

Spiritual people accomplish spiritual things.

# 6

# TRASH, FLOWERS AND FANFARE

*"God resists the proud, but gives grace to the humble. Humble yourselves in the sight of the Lord, and He will lift you up."—James 4:6, 10*

*"For I say, through the grace given to me, to everyone who is among you, not to think of himself more highly than he ought to think, but to think soberly, as God has dealt to each one a measure of faith."—Romans 12:3*

## 1993

Humility is a hard lesson to learn. It is easier to preach humility than to live it out. The Lord has a wonderful way of helping us grow in this area in the event that we ever get to a place of thinking of ourselves more highly than we ought. The Lord's heart is to "lift us up" as we humble ourselves before Him. I have learned this must be an active pursuit in our lives as Christians. We should never have to wonder if pride exists within us. We must always try to find its ugly head and pound it down like those "pop-up heads" arcade games. If not, I can assure you God will help us out.

Before going back home to the U.S., I thought it would be wonderful to take a few days off to help me unwind and relax. The family of one of my students from the mission school invited me to their house in the Ivory Coast. It was the perfect opportunity, and so I took this as God's answer to my prayer.

Cote d'Ivoire, as it is properly called, was much more developed than Liberia. The capital city, Abidjan, was very modern and had all of the amenities, such as running water and electricity. Those two things were enough to make the decision to experience another West African country and possibly get to enjoy some ice cream.

# LIVING PARABLE

My student contacted his family, and all was set for me to meet them at the airport and relax for about five days. I had only been to the airport of Cote d'Ivoire upon my travel to Liberia, so I was excited to see the city. Sure enough, four of his family members met me at the airport and we were off on another adventure. The first thing that hit me was that they had paved roads. I was not bouncing around trying to dodge potholes as in Liberia, nor was I rubbing shoulders with sweaty men and women, as our taxi had air conditioning. There were skyscrapers, sidewalks, highways and hotels. I absorbed every moment of the hour-long ride as if I had never seen these things before.

We drove around the city and eventually came to an area that looked very similar to my hometown in Florida. There were gated communities, nice houses and seemingly well-to-do people meeting on the streets, walking with their children and enjoying life. I even saw a person walking their dog on a leash. I had not seen that in Liberia because most of the dogs had 'disappeared' in the height of the war. Things were normal. I think that is what I remember most.

My student and his family were Liberian refugees living in Cote d'Ivoire, and they were wonderful people. As we got to know each other on this drive, I discovered that they were warm and welcoming and so grateful for the investment I had poured into their son.

"I've prepared your favorite Liberian dish," said the mother, a well-mannered and well-dressed woman, with perfectly styled hair and sparkling gold chains. In fact, all of them were dressed to the hilt. I leaned back in the front seat ready to enjoy my five-day vacation.

We drove through several nice neighborhoods on the outskirts of the city, which was lined with pristine houses, many of which were landscaped with colorful bougainvillea trees and tropical gardens. We continued driving until the road began to narrow, and we turned off onto a side street. These houses were much smaller, and the gardens had turned into tin cans that had become planters for small flowers sitting on windowsills. Then, we turned off the paved road and onto a dirt road. These houses were smaller still and reminded me more of Liberia.

# TRASH, FLOWERS AND FANFARE

The road narrowed further, and the smell of this area was putrefying. We were now dodging those familiar potholes. The taxi driver began to complain in French to the family as they nervously nudged his shoulder to press on. Maybe they could see my face displaying the concerns that were now in my mind. Had we gotten lost? This could not be the right place. This was the dump!

The taxi stopped in front of a small cinder block home. Most of the other houses in the area were made of tin sheets and sticks similar to pictures I had seen of the slums in Nairobi. The family got out of the back seat and began to talk to the driver in French. I stayed in the vehicle thinking we were lost, and that they were just seeking directions for getting back to the main road. To my surprise, the family was unloading my bags out of the trunk and asking me to come down.

I hesitated and all of a sudden got this unseemly feeling to go back to the airport. This was not the vacation spot my mind had projected for a five-day retreat before heading home. This was the city dump where they placed refugees who flooded into the country from Liberia when they had no place to go!

I tried to keep a stiff upper lip upon exiting the taxi. I wanted to get back in the car and ask the driver to take me to the Sofitel, a beautiful hotel that we had passed along the way. My student had told me that they had a nice home in Abidjan. He did not explain that it was nice only in comparison to the other homes in the same neighborhood.

Stepping onto the cement floor as we entered the house, I immediately noticed the decorations on the wall—a typical African calendar and some family pictures that seemed to be glued to the paint that covered the cinder blocks. Continuing a couple of steps further, I saw only plastic chairs in what appeared to be the family room. They walked me down a hot, dark corridor to show me to my room. Opening the door, I saw that my bed was a foam pad on the floor, and just above the pillow was a small opening for a window.

# LIVING PARABLE

It was obvious that the bed was made for a guest, yet I tried to continue in my state of denial hoping this was not my reality. They put my bags in the corner and asked me to follow them to the back door. Sure enough, my nostrils were not mistaken—the backyard was the city dump. The father began to explain how thankful he was that the Lord had provided this place for them when they had nowhere else to go. Rebels had forced them out of Liberia because of their tribal heritage, and he was amazed at God's provision for them in this strange land. I, on the other hand, was surprised that God would bring me here and was wondering if this was all a joke! This man acted as if his house was a palace on the French Riviera, while I was praying for deliverance.

After our meal, I excused myself and retired to my room. The heat was unbearable since we had to close the wood-framed shutter windows at night because of possible break-ins. I had built up such high expectations as to how the Lord would bless me because of all my labor for Him that year. I mean, I had been through a war, risked my life and surrendered all to follow Him. Surely I deserved to stay at the Sofitel. I was wrong—really wrong!

By the time of my departure, something had happened to my perspective. I had gotten to the place of gratitude and learned a lesson of faith by staying with this incredible family, though I was also thankful when that taxi pulled up to take me to the airport for my evening flight. They cried as I pulled away. I truly had fallen in love with this precious clan. They showed me a joy in the Lord despite their circumstances, and that humbled me.

As soon as the taxi dropped me off at the airport, I went to the bathroom for I was not feeling very well. Looking in the mirror, I noticed the whites of my eyes were slightly yellow and my skin was a strange color. In addition, my stomach was upset. I had not had a normal bowel movement since I left Florida over a year ago.

Upon boarding the airplane, I was slightly nauseous. My seat was located in the middle of the middle section. When I sat down, a large

# TRASH, FLOWERS AND FANFARE

Ivorian woman was on my right and a French businessman was on my left. Because of our language barrier, neither of them attempted to try to speak to me. I was not feeling well anyway and wholly concentrated on finding the nearest bathroom on the airplane.

Unfortunately for me, it was time to take off. Going down the runway, lifting up into the air and the pressure change in the cabin were all contributors to what would happen next in row 29. The seat belt sign was still on because we had not reached cruising altitude yet. Since those lights were only cautionary and nothing was tying me down to my seat, I politely asked the French man to allow me to pass. He would not move. I do not know if he did not move because he could not understand me or if he was simply being obstinate, but, in either case, I had to pass.

I forced my way into the aisle as the plane was still on the incline. Taking that last leap over the man in my way, my foot caught his foot, which caused me to lose my balance. Turning to catch myself before falling, my stomach hit the edge of the aisle seat opposite the row in which I was sitting. This blow was all my stomach needed to declare, "I have had enough!"

Without warning, I violently sprayed the contents of my dinner onto the laps of the three women innocently sitting in their seats. Unable to care about the commotion I created in row 29, I desperately headed to the bathroom. It seemed as though the whole plane was staring at me, wondering if I would lose it again. Every step was a risk, but I had to keep walking despite how I felt for at that moment the airplane latrine was the answer to all of my problems.

I did not want to leave the bathroom. The flight attendant was saying something in French as she knocked on the door. It did not sound very compassionate, and since I was busy cleaning myself up, I decided to take my time. When I finally opened the door, I peeked out to see if anyone was looking. Of course, everyone was looking. Down the aisle, I could see the three Ivorian women still cleaning themselves from my personal catastrophe. I was completely humiliated, but I knew I had to walk back to my seat.

My clothes were wet from attempting to clean them, and I was sure I had somewhat of an odor about me. However, in my mind it did not warrant the two people sitting next to me to suck their teeth and turn their backs to shun me—well, maybe it did.

The next fourteen hours of travel were horrific. I was violently sick the entire way home and had apparently caught something during my five-day vacation at the dump. I had never been more grateful to hear, "Welcome to Fort Lauderdale" over the loud speaker than I was at the moment we landed. To top it off, Andrea and my family were waiting in the lobby with signs and banners as if welcoming a war-wearied vet. With much wisdom, my parents had planned a time for us to get away before the craziness of life ensued. Within a few days, my parents, Andrea and I traveled to North Carolina to a small cabin they have in the mountains.

I have found in my personal walk with the Lord that there is something about the mountains when meeting with Him. Just as He had brought Moses and Elijah to the mountain, I felt He had brought me there so that I could hear His voice of comfort, direction and instruction.

I was shell-shocked upon my arrival home. From the war, to the dump, then to the mountains—all in a matter of days. My mind was whirling from everything, from judgment of those living the American way to sorrow for the ones I had left behind. I had to regain context for the culture I had repatriated.

"Chet, when you are in Liberia, be a Liberian," my mom said. "When you are in the States, be an American. Become all things to all men. This is not our problem to deal with; it is yours."

Such wisdom.

Andrea was caught in the middle of my mental struggles. She desperately wanted to be there for me; however, she also had needs of her own, which she purposed to lay aside on almost every occasion.

# TRASH, FLOWERS AND FANFARE

One day we were walking through a field of flowers on the side of a mountain. It truly was an incredibly romantic moment. Andrea had taken a few steps ahead of me, and she turned to look at me. That's when I noticed tears in her eyes.

"What's the matter?" I asked her, baffled by her crumpled face. It was a beautiful sunny day without a cloud in the sky. The temperature was perfect, and looking at the colors of the flowers was like viewing a kaleidoscope. *What in the world could be wrong?* I thought.

She gathered her thoughts and emotions and said, "You are supposed to bend down, pick up a bouquet of flowers and give them to me."

*Are you kidding me?* I thought to myself.

Please, remember my context. I had just come out of war and had been in survival mode for so long that I had become functional and pragmatic.

I looked at her and politely said, "Andrea, if you want a flower, simply bend down and pick it up yourself."

I did not realize at the moment that I had said something wrong until her gentle eyes flooded with tears. Let me assure you that we had strong fellowship that day. And let me assure you that I have grown since then. Andrea has done well in training me over the last twenty years, and now fresh flowers are commonplace in our home.

There was no vacation or fanfare upon my arrival home, even though I had presumed that people would want to hear about all my adventures. Yet, life had gone on without me, and everyone was preoccupied with their own experiences and challenges. This is not to say that no one cared, for that would be a misrepresentation of the truth. In essence, we are all His servants, doing what is our duty. For some it may be teaching Sunday school, while for others it may be the mission field; yet for all of us, it is simply our duty.

Peter reminds us that God opposes the proud. In some sense, it is strange to think that a loving God would come against us for any reason. Yet the truth of Scripture is that He will not share His glory with another. In this, it is important to remember that God disciplines the son He loves.

## LIVING PARABLE

He humbles you when you are prideful, only to lift you up so that your heart is in a place where you will let your light so shine before men for others to see your good works and glorify your Father in heaven. Our daily plight is to humble ourselves; His constant desire is to lift us up.

# NO MORE MONEY!

*"Now faith is the substance of things hoped for,
the evidence of things not seen."—Hebrews 11:1*

*"But if we hope for what we do not see,
we eagerly wait for it with perseverance." —Romans 8:25*

## 1994-1995

We were at the airport preparing to leave for Liberia, and on my back, in one of those convoluted carriers, was four-month-old Micaiah, our firstborn son. Before walking through the security line, Andrea and I said goodbye to everyone who came to see us off.

I was surprised to see my parents at the airport. It had been a very hard six months prior to our departure. They were struggling to understand why we would not wait until Micaiah was a little older before we took him into a war-torn country. Since he was their first grandson, they wanted to protect him from the dangers that could lie ahead. Andrea's parents were not as vocal but had definitely expressed their concerns as well, and they were not the only ones articulating their opinions.

We attended a church of several thousand people, and our pastor brought us to the platform to lay hands on us before sending us out. After the service, a gentleman, whom I had never seen before, walked up to me. He began to detail his concerns about the country of Liberia because it was in the middle of civil war. He intensely questioned my call. The conversation seemed to be getting heated from his end, even though I continued to assure him that Jesus was with us and guiding us to press on.

# LIVING PARABLE

Finally, he looked at me and said, "You're one of the most selfish people I have ever met. It is unheard of that you would take your wife and small child into such danger and have no regard for their lives."

I wanted to defend myself but knew that there was no point in trying to persuade him. I wish he had been in my car earlier that week when the Lord had challenged my faith in an "Abrahamic" way. My devotions had been in Genesis, and I was thinking about the sacrifices made by the patriarchs of our faith. With a still small voice, the Lord asked me, "Are you willing to lay down your life?"

I responded with confidence, "Of course, Lord."

He then asked, "What of Andrea's life?"

I hesitated to respond and said silently, "Yes, Lord."

As I drove further down the road, the Lord came to me one last time. "And what of Micaiah's life?"

I pulled off the road in tears. This was too much and I was unable to answer. I said, "Lord, it is not natural to lose a son."

He said, "I know."

Despite all of these thoughts and emotions, I had a peace that passed understanding. I was confident the Lord would protect us, and my wife was beside me in this new venture of faith. Andrea and I had been married a little over a year at this point. We had decided that we would not go on the field until after our first year of marriage. Our desire was that we would grow together first and then head out. This was a good decision because our first year of marriage required a lot of attending.

Andrea had become settled with the decision to move to Liberia. She had conceived three weeks after our wedding, and the pregnancy was very difficult. Her morning sickness turned into afternoon and evening sickness as well. In fact, we began to call it "anytime sickness," for it seemed that she was never relieved of the nausea caused by the pregnancy. I had to keep reminding her that this was a production, not a sickness. Four months after we were married, we took a vision trip to Liberia. I thought it would be a good idea for Andrea to get a taste of her future life. It was rough.

# NO MORE MONEY!

Andrea got sick on the plane, in the taxi, at the house, in the market or anywhere she stepped foot. The smells would set her off, and it seemed she was allergic to the people, the country and the idea of ever returning.

When we got back to the States, Andrea and I would go on evening walks, as the exercise was good for the pregnancy. I could tell that she had something she wanted to discuss on one particular evening, so I started the conversation with small talk.

I tried to laugh about some of our experiences in Liberia. I reminded her of the time we were walking on the beach one night on our way home from dinner with a friend. We were staring at the stars and talking about what life would be like when we lived in the country for good.

All of a sudden, Andrea was gone. The river had forged a ravine in the sand, and Andrea did not see the ledge and simply fell over into the water. Her fall stopped my forward movement, and I looked down the five to six-foot drop to see my wife hysterically laughing in the water.

I stepped down into the ravine to help her up, and she continued to laugh. We climbed the other side of the cut, and Andrea continued in her hysteria. In fact, she laughed all the way home. We retold the story to our hosts, and she laughed all the more.

Even as we were getting ready for bed, she would burst into spontaneous merriment at the thought of what had happened earlier that evening. I was beginning to get a little concerned. I have since realized that on that night, Andrea found a happy place that I had wished to find for a long time; and might I add, still hope to find.

Unfortunately, the memory of slipping into that ravine did not amuse her on our walk that evening. She seemed pointed, somewhat agitated, and felt compelled to tell me, "I do not feel called to Liberia."

I was discouraged and hurt. Every bit of my being could not wait to get back, and now the woman I had married did not want to go. Frustrated, I said, "Then you married the wrong man."

We walked home in silence and went to bed without saying much. Knowing where my wife was mentally, all I could do was pray. We were not arguing over the point any longer, but I could tell that Andrea was still working through what it meant to surrender all. I had the same struggle, but for some reason, it looked worse on her than it did on me. I judged her instead of dealing with the issue in my own life.

To add to the internal, spiritual turmoil, I remember having my devotions one morning and reading, "Provide neither gold nor silver nor copper in your money belts, nor bag for your journey, nor two tunics, nor sandals, nor staff, for a worker is worthy of his food" (Matthew 10:9-10).

As I pondered this verse, I sensed the Lord telling me not to raise support but to simply go to Liberia and trust Him for our provision. With all of the insecurity that Andrea was experiencing, how in the world was I to communicate this as a measure of comfort that the Lord was truly sending us? All I could do was pray!

One evening, Andrea cooked dinner for us. Her meals were always an adventure, as she was learning to cook. I was not very graceful in my attempt to encourage her for I often would come into the kitchen and say things like, "Is something burning?"

We have grown so much together in grace that I am surprised I was the man I used to be, but I am grateful that He who began the work is still not finished.

We did not talk much over dinner since everything in our lives revolved around getting to Liberia, and the imminent future had become more functional than spiritual. That is not to say that we were not in prayer or seeking God regarding our plans. It was more the condition of our marriage, and the conversation we had on the night of that walk. As we finished our meal, I knew it was time to broach the topic and went straight for the jugular by announcing, "I believe the Lord has told me that we are not to raise support and sell all that we have and move to Liberia."

*Whew!* I did it. At this point, I should probably remind everyone that I was only twenty-four years old. In no way would I recommend the above behavior in a marital counseling session as the technique to approach spiritual concerns in your marriage. In fact, I would probably use that story to describe what not to do and how to learn from my failure. In any case, it was on the table, and we were forced to deal with it.

Andrea looked at me for quite a while. Her face was no longer pointed, but tender. She looked almost relieved that I had brought up Liberia and appeared anxious to talk and tell me some things that were on her heart. Her look and demeanor pulled me in because she seemed to honor what God had spoken to me and said in return, "Chet, I believe the Lord spoke the same thing to me."

My mouth dropped.

This was the first time I had heard my wife say that God had spoken positively to her about Liberia since we had left the country earlier that summer. Only a month or so had passed, and she had purposely pursued the Lord to change either her heart or mine. She had not nagged me on the issue or even dropped hints of her concern, but simply took it to the Lord in prayer.

"The Lord ministered similar verses to me earlier this week, but I was not sure how to come and tell you," said Andrea.

This practice of prayer would teach me and train her to understand that it is our lifeline connection to the direction of God for every step in our lives. We were both growing in our relationship together, and this moment—which I can say was a turning point in our marriage—catapulted our connection. No longer would we 'play' faith. We had determined that day to 'live' faith with each other and purpose to please God. Being on the same page made us stronger, and we were able to move forward in peace.

At the same time, God was doing a work in one of my dearest friends, Kenny Engels. He and his wife, Christi, were living in Germany at the time. He was a 'super-model' in Europe and lived there for several months out of the year. We had met as teenagers in the ministry of Campus Life. Completely different from each other, God forged a friendship between us that has remained strong until this day.

# LIVING PARABLE

Growing up, we did almost everything together. From surfing to traveling, to rebelling and more, he was always my hero and still is today. He became the older brother I never had, and his family truly became my own. My teenage years were enriched because of the way they loved me. Today, we have tried to model our lives to embrace anyone who comes through our doors as this family did for me.

Kenny and Christi believed that the Lord was calling them to Liberia as well. I had done everything I could to dissuade them. In fact, I wrote a four-page, handwritten letter at one time explaining the nightmare of living in Liberia. I figured that if I could convince them not to go, maybe they were not called. Through it all, they persevered and planned to travel with us in order to serve the Lord and fulfill their calling. Needless to say, I was blessed beyond measure and could not believe my brother would be with me on this journey.

The time was approaching for us to travel. The next step for us involved purchasing our plane tickets. Our pastor had told us that he would buy them for us as a gift from the church, so we contacted our travel agent and arranged the itinerary for the upcoming journey. The monies were due on a Monday, as we had booked the travel the previous Friday.

Over the weekend, my responsibility at the church was to handle all of the events of the Sunday night service, including the children's ministry, janitorial services and general service oversight. I remember that our pastor was gradually going through the book of Psalms. Little did I know that Sunday nights had become a training ground for me in regards to worship, administration and management. I have discovered in life that our heavenly coach, Jesus, is always training us. That weekend, my pastor came up to me and said, "Chet, I don't think we are going to pay for your ticket. Watch the Lord work!"

*What?* I was confused.

*How could you not follow through on your commitment?* I wanted to ask. I mean, doesn't the Word explain that our "yes is yes, and our no is no"? I could not believe that he told me this and went home to Andrea very upset. That night we counted the money we had at home. The day before, we had held a garage sale to get rid of all of our things and made a whopping $330. The money for the ticket was due on Monday, and we were about $1200 short of our goal. As we were going through our wallets to see what else we had, I noticed several checks in Andrea's purse. I took them out. They were written to our church.

"What are these?" I asked her.

"They're our tithe checks over the past several months," she said.

The checks did not add up to much, but she was concerned about turning them in as we were always running short in our monthly bills.

"Hand them in and let's trust the Lord for His provision," I told her. On our way home from church that day, we were in prayer about how to pay our airfare. There was nothing we could do. I was still not very pleased with our pastor and began to wonder if the church was in some kind of financial crisis. We decided to stop at our post office box on the way home to see if we had any mail. There was one parcel from my friend Kenny. I was excited to get something from him, as he had been away in Europe for some time. He always had a word of encouragement to say, but I believe this was one of the first letters he had ever written me.

When I opened the letter, there was not much written on the sheet of paper. However, inside that envelope was a check for almost the exact amount we needed in order to purchase our tickets. In fact, it was about $330 short. With this check and our garage sale, God had provided for us on the exact day we needed it. Tickets were purchased. God was glorified. I find it amazing how the Lord used our efforts and His Spirit to accomplish His work. Kenny was moved by the Spirit to send a contribution while we were moved in obedience to sell all that we had. Jesus instigated the entire plan in both of our hearts, and His will was accomplished. We landed in Liberia with this story of faith. It provided courage and strength for us to trust Him while we were there.

# LIVING PARABLE

Within a few days of our arrival, people back home began to support our endeavor. We had not raised support and only had enough money in our account to rent our home, set up house and begin life in Liberia. We had purposed together that we would use our savings for the work of the ministry and quickly realized that it would soon run out.

Around the second month, we had the money for the third month. In the third, we had enough for the fourth. For three years it continued in this manner as God provided manna from above. Our heart was that as long as the Lord provided, we would continue to serve Him in this foreign land. Around the sixth month, we began to understand why the Lord had provided for us in this way.

Liberia was hard. In fact, it is best explained through the lens of another young man who joined us for the first few months. I will never forget how he barged into our room one night and had had enough.

"A mosquito came into the room and tried to pick up my leg and carry it outside to my friends to suck every ounce of blood out of it!" He said in jest. We laughed, but he was not far from the truth! Because of the intense conditions, we wanted to go home. Andrea and I began having serious conversations about returning. Micaiah looked like a big red bump from either ant or mosquito bites. Andrea had perpetual diarrhea. I was trying to plant a church in the face of much opposition, and we just figured that it was too much. Then, another check would come.

We started praying for the money to stop. We had made the commitment that we would stay as long as the funds were there, so we figured our well would soon run dry and looked forward with great expectation to having no money in the bank. I know this seems opposite to most people's aspirations, but if you were living in Liberia at the time, you would completely understand. To our great disappointment, the money would be there every month. Sooner rather than later, we began to realize that God was holding us to our commitment and knew how to keep us there. There was nothing we could do. He was in complete control. When the money ran out three years later, we came home. Amazing how that worked out.

# 8

# MISSIONARY OR MERCENARY

*"The steps of a good man are ordered by the Lord, and He delights in his way.*
*Though he fall, he shall not be utterly cast down;*
*for the Lord upholds him with His hand."—Psalm 37:23-24*

## 1996

There were two things of which I was sure: God had called me to Liberia to plant churches and to minister to child soldiers. Oftentimes people will ask me, "How did you know what God was calling you to do or where He was calling you to go?" I understand their plea, as I had this same question before I left to go on the field.

Andrea and I took a trip to Washington DC in search of the answer to that question. We interviewed several missionaries on our journey, and even had the privilege to stay with a couple that were shepherds in Virginia. The experience opened our eyes to the reason why Jesus calls us sheep. In fact, if you are a church leader, I encourage you to visit a sheep farm, as it will enlighten the manner in which you need to care for the sheep God has entrusted you with. If you are unable to get that opportunity, read Phillip Keller's book, *A Shepherd Looks at Psalm 23*.

Andrea and I discovered that every missionary had a different answer for how they knew God had directed and placed them in their calling. The only chorus line we noticed was that each person had an intimate relationship with Jesus. They were people of the Word, followed wise counsel and had an assortment of confirmation that were specific to each individual. In other words, God knows how to get His point across to His people to do His work! Don't worry about the answer. Simply seek the Master. He will be faithful to add this unto you.

# LIVING PARABLE

The Lord showed us in Matthew 16 that He was building His church. We figured that if that is what He is about, we should be about building the church as well. He had explained that we should "go into all the world." Therefore, as Liberia was in my path, I assumed that was His direction. He had used Luke 4 to explain that He had "sent Me to heal the brokenhearted." I knew the children who had been caught in the conflict of civil war in this country needed to be healed.

During that time, I had a distinct dream. I was reading a newspaper and it suddenly started spinning. It would stop spinning, as in those old time movies, and I would read a headline. Then, it would start spinning again to get to the next headline, as if moving me along in a story. Finally, the last headline I remember was, "Missionary Saves Rebels' Lives." On the front page of that paper, there was a picture of me shaking the hand of a young rebel soldier.

Then, I woke up.

For six months, we worked diligently at planting the church in the capital city. Ultimately, our plan was to move into the interior of Liberia and get back to the mission I had visited when I was fourteen years old. Unfortunately, the war was heavy in that area, and there was no way for us to move there until the roads opened allowing for free passage. We purposed to move from place to place as the roads opened along the way, getting closer to our goal.

With this in mind, we determined to plant churches everywhere the Lord moved us. While reading the book of Acts, I discovered that in every town to which Paul was directed, he planted a church and set up leaders before moving to the next place. I used this as an instruction manual without making things much more complicated than the simplicity of the Word.

We got news that the road had opened to the city of Buchanan. Often known as the "second city" of Liberia, it is really no bigger than a large town. Located on the coast, it is a port city from which companies would export iron ore, logs and various natural resources. A railway from the interior ran to Buchanan carrying mostly the iron ore that was mined from the mountains.

# MISSIONARY OR MERCENARY

Liberia is rich in resources, and for this reason you can begin to see why warlords fought for its control. I had not been to this city for almost ten years. We had no idea what to expect along the road, but after much prayer, we believed it was our next step of faith. Therefore, I, along with two other missionaries and two Liberians, chartered a car and began the journey.

The road was littered with as many as eighteen checkpoints along the road to Buchanan. Each one required all passengers to exit the vehicle for a painstaking inspection, including our bags. Once you were thoroughly frisked, you walked a winding path to reach the other side, much like the security line at an airport. Doing this eighteen times can begin to wear on you!

I saw burn marks on the road, and so I asked our driver, "What are these?"

"That's where they burn the bodies found on the road, instead of burying them," he said.

The grim reality of how many people had died in this war surrounded us. Since I had been living in the capital city, I had not seen the complete impact of the war, or come into contact with combat, rebels, and intense military zones. Every checkpoint seemed to intensify the closer we got to Buchanan. On a paved road the trip took about an hour and a half. However, due to war, the road was mostly destroyed, and so this trip took close to six hours.

There were potholes as long and deep as our vehicle. Various mud bogs slowed our pace to a halt on several occasions, and between checkpoints, we were forced to get out of the chartered car numerous times and push our way out of the sludge in which we had gotten trapped.

Villages along the road had been decimated. Buildings had been burned and looted of everything from the roofs to the copper wire in the walls. Weeds and grass crept onto the road like an old ghost town, and people were few and far between. Most of the government structures had profane drawings and script that I will refrain from describing.

# LIVING PARABLE

Various threats were posted on personal homes, while roadside farms appeared overgrown and unkempt.

As we approached the center point known as the #1 Compound, our driver began to warn us to remain calm. Six pairs of eyes stared back at him. We were sweating profusely in a crowded, older model Toyota Corolla, which did nothing to improve our predicament or hot disposition. Getting out of the car at the various checkpoints had served as an oasis stop-n-go! This by no means was a type of service center in the middle of a structured highway, but the cool breeze did refresh our faces and the quick stop allowed us to stretch our legs, letting the blood start flowing again.

There were many cars parked at this checkpoint. The peacekeepers were not letting many of the vehicles or people pass. This stop was also much different than the previous ones. There was actually a desk at which everyone had to register in order to keep moving forward. The soldiers were from Nigeria, and it seemed like they were having a bad day.

One soldier in particular was loud and obnoxious. He sat behind a desk as he directed everyone with an iron fist. Clearly, he was in charge. All of the other soldiers quickly followed his commands.

"That is Sergeant Pa Sergeant," said our driver, pointing in his direction.

"What's his name?" I asked, not sure I had heard right.

"Sergeant Pa Sergeant," he said, with a tremor in his voice. I heard the name this time, including the fear factor behind every syllable.

"Drop!" The standing soldier gave us the familiar command, and instantly we all got out of the vehicle.

One of the missionaries turned to me and said, "I want to speak to one of the soldiers."

"I don't think that's a good idea," I said.

"I am filled with the Holy Spirit and feel the need to communicate," he said, and before I knew it, he was walking toward Sergeant Pa Sergeant.

Sergeant was probably close to fifty years of age. He had the traditional scarring marks on his face that Nigerian boys receive at an early age. He was worn and weary from war. And from where I was standing, I could see nothing pleasant about either his tone or his demeanor. In fact, his speech sounded more like an angry, barking dog than a human being. And my friend was walking briskly straight to him.

Sergeant Pa Sergeant looked directly at this white man. The expression on his face told a story, mainly, that he was caught off guard. I am sure the only white people he had seen in this region were part of a UN convoy, not coming out of a broken-down taxi. Sergeant looked past my friend and glanced at the rest of us—a group of white people standing at his checkpoint.

"Who are you?" He said as he suddenly turned his attention to the white man in front of him.

"I am a missionary," my friend responded politely.

"A mercenary?" Sergeant asked, and immediately I knew we were in trouble.

"Yes, a missionary," said my friend, who didn't quite understand the Nigerian's broken English. Lesser wars have been started over such communication blunders, but it appeared as if we had just initiated World War III.

Sergeant stood up instantly.

"Who brought these mercenaries to my checkpoint?" He demanded to know, as he violently walked in our direction. Everyone, including myself, began to cower with each step he took.

Without hesitation, he took his bamboo stick in his hand and hit Jerome, a Liberian friend who traveled with us, on the top of the head and had him lie down in the sun. The three white guys were gathered, and our interrogation began. Sergeant Pa Sergeant had become judge and jury. Unfortunately for us, he thought he already had a confession that we were mercenaries. I prayed.

Our driver was told to go on ahead as we would be detained. Jerome was still lying in the sun, and none of us were sure of our fate. I could not believe we were in this situation and tried to talk to Sergeant to no avail. Several minutes later, we were escorted to an abandoned house. Thankfully, Sergeant was accountable to superior officers. Inside, there was a table, two chairs and no other furniture. Two commanding officers presented themselves upon our arrival. They appeared well-dressed, well-mannered, and respectable.

I did not realize it then, but we were being placed on trial. The soldier who escorted us to the building began to press his case against us. I listened intently and asked the Lord for wisdom as to what to say. The only thing that kept coming to mind were the words of Jesus to His disciples, when He said that we should not worry about what to say when we are put in front of magistrates because the Holy Spirit would faithfully give us words at that time.

I began to defend our case by communicating the truth of what happened. One of the officers pleasantly smiled as he heard the case and realized by simply looking at us that we had no idea what we were doing. I am sure he assumed the truth of our ignorance and innocence by our demeanor, and let us go.

I walked outside to my fellow comrades whose heads were bowed in weariness from the heat of the sun. We were free to go, but freedom always has responsibilities attached to it. We had no transportation, and Buchanan was thirty-five to forty miles away. With no other options, we walked along the road.

Within a few minutes, a UN vehicle passed and stopped, bewildered at the sight of three white men walking on the side of the road with two Liberians. They had enough space for three, so I placed them inside the air-conditioned car, and off they went like kings in their palanquin.

Jerome and I continued to walk on the side of the road.

"We are just going to have to sleep on the road," I said. "There is no turning back."

Jerome nodded.

Despite all of these obstacles, I knew it was the best decision. Besides, I had sent my three friends ahead of me and could not abandon them, though I felt abandoned by the Lord.

# MISSIONARY OR MERCENARY

*Where are you?* I prayed, but there was no answer.

About an hour later, an armored vehicle towing a missile slowed down behind us. They had stopped to relieve themselves, and so I asked, "Can you give us a ride?"

Surprisingly, they agreed. As I went to get in the vehicle, one of the soldiers put his finger up and pointed to the trailer in the back. I looked and wondered what he was communicating. However, there was no confusion in his tone or direction. The ride they were offering was on the missile. Jerome and I got on the trailer and hugged the ammunition the whole way to Buchanan. With every bounce and pothole, I wondered when this thing would explode or take off. I could not believe this missile had become my chariot; however, I was grateful to no longer be walking. It is amazing the things you can get used to and consider normal when you never would have dreamed of being a part of such things.

When we arrived in the city, the soldiers took us to the main part of town. It felt as if every eye was fixed on me. First and foremost, I was white. Secondly, I was hugging a missile. What a powerful way to make your entrance as a missionary! I'm not sure they teach you how to deal with that one at seminary.

I was only a teenager when I had last visited this town. I had no idea where to go, but I knew whom I wanted to see. Prior to making the journey to Buchanan, the Lord led me to a friend who lived in Monrovia to discuss my plans to go further into the interior for the sake of the gospel. As I was sharing with her, she communicated to me that she knew a man with a similar heart to mine. His name was Sylvester Williams.

She described Mr. Williams as an older man who had been through many trials in the war. Everyone had a horrific story, yet according to her, his was one of the worst. She explained that Mr. Williams had a limp, was about five foot nine inches, and lived near 'Otis Spot,' somewhere just off the main road in Buchanan.

It was late, and the sun was beginning to set by the time we finally caught up with our friends. We had no place to sleep and everyone was hungry.

# LIVING PARABLE

"Is there a hotel nearby?" We asked several people and were directed to a guest house that was "...down this road, turn left at the big tree, take the small path to the old mission school, and go straight ahead from there." A GPS would have been nice. We spent the rest of the fading day getting settled and meeting for prayer. The guesthouse seemed to be an abandoned building with foam pads on the ground, but none of us seemed to care. We were thankful this day had come to an end, in a peaceful way. The next morning, we were up early and began our search for Mr. Williams.

"Do you know Mr. Williams?" We asked the lady who kept us for the night, but she had never heard of him.

"Do you know where we can find Mr. Williams?" We asked some people on the street, but they had never heard of him either. For as popular as my friend in Monrovia had told me he was, it seemed as though no one knew him in this town. I began to get suspicious. We were on the main road, when we came upon a Lebanese merchant.

"Do you know Mr. Williams?" I asked and he nodded, directing us to Otis Spot, where we found his house.

"He's in the bush making coal," his children said, and the last words filled us with disappointment. "And he won't be back for several days."

Still, I left some funds for him to come to us in Monrovia, where we could meet. Several days later, Mr. Williams arrived on our front porch in Monrovia, and we hit it off immediately. He was a light-hearted and seemingly gentle older man. Clearly, well educated, Mr. Williams had either information or an opinion about any topic we discussed. Our whole family fell in love with him, and after only a few days of his visit, we were calling him "Grandpa Syl."

"Please, explain your story," I asked him one night and before he began, he looked to the ground and held up his leg.

Grandpa Syl was a very strong man, yet he had a significant limp. He carefully explained, "In the heat of the war, my son and I were traveling back to Buchanan from Monrovia in the back of a large truck. When we were only about thirty minutes away from Buchanan, we started hearing shooting sounds, and I realized that we were caught in an ambush. I looked over and saw that my son had been shot in the back, and at the same time, the truck began to topple into a ditch on the side of the road. I was tossed from the truck and was lying in my own pool of blood, as my leg had been shot seven times."

Grandpa Syl paused for a moment. He looked to the wall as his lips pursed, and he stayed turned to it absently. There wasn't a sound, as if the house had winked into darkness and only his agonizing memory was left. We waited, looking at him with suppressed eagerness.

As he cleared his voice, I saw a shift in his eyes, and I understood it. He had put that single, heart piercing, calling to mind on hold so that he could continue telling his story.

"I looked over and there was a woman walking around completely confused," he said after a moment. "She was holding her skirt up folded over as if she was carrying something and all of a sudden, she fell over dead. When she fell to the ground, I could see that she was holding her insides, as she had been cut across the stomach."

Andrea gasped as he recounted the event, and I wondered what had happened to him.

"The rebels came up to me and saw me lying in my blood. Hearing other soldiers coming up through the woods, they ran off and left me there to die. I remained in that ditch for seven days. Maggots began to fester in my wound, but God was actually using them to save my life. Then, the same group of rebels that had shot us down came back to the site and saw me still alive."

One of them said to him, "Pape, you still alive? You won't die in this war."

Grandpa Syl remembered how they had walked away, and that it was strange to think that rebels would prophesy over his life.

"In either case, I am still here," he said admittedly. "I closed my eyes and fell into a deep sleep. I had no water or food for seven days. My leg was rotten, and I began to think that my time had come."

Then, he had a dream. In his dream, he was getting ready to cross the Jordan when an angel came to him and said, "It is not your time. Go back and serve the Lord."

The next thing he knew, an old woman was wakening him. "She dragged me out of the ditch and cared for me until my leg was better. I made a commitment to the Lord that I would serve Him all of my days, and so, here I am today."

There was not a dry eye in the house that night. God had sent us this man and prepared him in the most unique way to develop a heart for the oppressor that almost cost him his life. The budding of our relationship had begun, and from that moment on, Grandpa Syl helped guide, lead, and direct all of our endeavors to reach child soldiers in Liberia.

I am forever grateful.

# CLOAKS AND TUNICS

*"Though I am free from all men, I have made myself a servant to all, that I might win the more."–1 Corinthians 9:19*

## 1996

I was jolted out of bed by a blood-curdling scream around 1 a.m. Without hesitation I reached over our straw mattress to check on Andrea, but she was not there. My heart started racing, and I charged through the bedroom door toward the sound that had awakened me.

Our bathroom was located at the other end of the hallway just outside our bedroom door. As I raced down the corridor, I saw Andrea coming out of the bathroom with her hands in the air. Her eyes were wet with tears, but she was laughing. By this time, everyone in the house was awake.

There were close to twenty people living with us at the time. We had moved to Buchanan in our attempt to discover where we believed God was leading us. As typical of a traditional Liberian home, the wealthy would take in other children and family members to avoid the stigma of selfishness. Because we were Americans, everyone thought we were rich. Therefore, we followed suit and brought in other children to combat the cultural perception of stinginess.

Practically, this was a safety measure as well. Buchanan was different from Monrovia. We were much closer to rebel territory, and security was limited at best. Having ten young Liberian men living in the home was like Abraham having 318 fighting men with him to combat the forces of five kings. It was just smart!

"Is everything all right?" I asked immediately.

Andrea nodded.

# LIVING PARABLE

She was in the hallway holding a candle as our only light. Suddenly, everyone surrounded her, as she described with laughter what had just happened.

"I woke up to go to the bathroom," she said. "As I sat on the toilet, I saw a rat crawling across the sill of the door. I hit the door, and the rat jumped in my direction." Hence, the blood-curdling scream. In the middle of her story, one of the young boys in the house began to yell, "Rogue! Rogue! Rogue!" We had become familiar with that term because of the constant security breach in Buchanan. This term was used to describe someone stealing or breaking into your home.

One neighbor would shout trying to awaken all the other neighbors, hoping that this alarm system would prevent the rogue from stealing. Usually, these rogues were rebel soldiers that would come into Buchanan in the middle of the night to steal and then return to their forces in the bush by day. We had become so accustomed to this routine that quite often we would go to bed early, wake up at midnight and stay awake until four, on guard for whoever might try to break in that evening.

Every one of us ran to the sound of the alarm. Sure enough, two men were escaping out of our garage door as we spied them from the window. For some reason, the boys all ran to the front door and ran outside. I followed suit, thinking this was the wisest thing to do at that moment since everyone else was doing it. Unfortunately, because I was the last to exit, I did not see in what direction the boys ran and went the opposite way.

It was pitch black. When the moon does not shine in Liberia and the clouds cover the stars, you cannot see your hand in front of your face. All of a sudden, I heard the scampering of feet like that of a herd of cattle running toward me. One of the guys yelled, "He's got a gun!"

My feet reacted before my mind engaged, and I ran to the front door for safety. We had just shut and bolted the door when the two thugs who had tried to break in reached our front porch.

"Get out!" We yelled loudly as we braced the door.

They left.

# CLOAKS AND TUNICS

By the grace of God, we were saved. We sat in our living room for the rest of the night endlessly repeating the story from different perspectives. Andrea constantly chimed in, "Praise God for the rat that caused me to scream!"

I guess if God can use a donkey for Balaam, He is more than welcome to use a rat for us. This was life in Buchanan.

In fact, I'll never forget one night when it was raining. In this region, it could very well be either a blessing or a curse. In one sense, it cooled the night and made for a good rest. On the other hand, rogues would take advantage of this and purpose to break in. Heavy storms were even worse. Because our roofs were made of aluminum sheets, the sound of the water hitting the tin could drown out the noise of someone cutting through the iron bars on our windows. Got to give it to these guys...they are good!

Through several storms, we would sit in various places of the house to guard windows and doors. One evening, I was assigned to the dining room. There was a large eight-foot window on the back wall. I would sit below the window and look through it on occasion to discover if there was any activity. The storms are violent in Liberia. Heavy rain, boisterous thunder and streaks of lightning that made the night seem as day were terrifying to Micaiah, who was almost one year old at the time.

Every five minutes or so, I would take a glimpse to secure my area of the house. Kneeling on the ground, I peeked into the dark night and could not see a thing outside the window. The rain was beating so heavily that water was coming into the house through the slatted windowpanes. Thunder roared and lightning followed.

When the sky was lit, I was no longer looking into darkness but straight into the eyes of several men who were trying to break into our home. I yelled as loud as I could. Startled by my appearance, the men on the other side shrieked and ran away. These occurrences became a normal part of our daily routine. God was supernaturally protecting us, as He did with the shouts of Joshua at the walls of Jericho.

# LIVING PARABLE

It may seem strange, but we actually liked Buchanan more than Monrovia. The pace was slower, the people were friendly and it had more of a 'hometown' feel than the busy capital city. Despite the challenges we faced in this town, I think the Lord had simply settled our hearts and given us a peace that passes understanding, since we were following His lead each step of the way.

Ministry was different in Buchanan. In the States we were used to sports, youth and young adult ministries for which you plan an activity, people show up, a Bible study is given, and a prayer is offered. In Buchanan, ministry was about survival. About 200 yards from our home was a displacement camp. These were horrific places that festered death and disease.

Constructed by the UN for temporary housing, thousands of people would live in four-by-four matted structures with blue tarps as roofs. This was not living; it was survival. These people had come from all over Liberia. Rebels took over their lands and forced them to leave, join the rebel forces or die. Most people facing this choice left. In order to accommodate the migration into the major cities, the UN built these displacement centers to house the influx of people. They were never meant for long-term care, but as the war raged on, no one was willing to leave and face certain death.

We planted a church very close to the displacement center. This provided us the opportunity to open a small clinic and provide for physical needs as best we could. It seemed that almost every night we would have someone in our home from the center that was deathly ill with some kind of disease. It was exasperating; there was always someone in need.

I began to realize why Paul said for us to "...not grow weary in doing good" (Galatians 6:9). It can be a challenge at times. Therefore, staying connected with the Source of our strength became vital in order for us to press on. So many people were coming to Christ; the Lord had opened a great and effective door. We began to see that though we could not go into the interior, the people from the interior could come to us. The church was growing tremendously, and we had services on Sunday and Wednesday. We had the opportunity to start discipleship classes and even a choir.

Once a month, we would host a baptism down at the water's edge and see ten to twenty people be obedient to the Lord in baptism. The waterfront was sketchy at best. In many places around our planet, city lights grow brighter as the earth lurches away from the sun, reflecting its glow on the water. Not in Africa. It is dark, African river water. Often, as I was baptizing people, I would be silently praying for protection for myself. The thought that something could be lurking or swimming around me, and even trying to get in me was never far from my mind.

The baptisms were such a joy, though. Liberians love to sing harmonious choruses that sound like angelic choirs. After we were finished, they would sing all the way home rejoicing in the Lord for what He had done. The water was located on the other side of the displacement camp. Thus, the sound of singing would ring through the camp as we walked through it on our way home.

One morning, our singing was abruptly stopped when a woman who was crying uncontrollably accosted us. Weeping bitterly, she fell to the ground in front of our entourage and rolled in the dirt, refusing to be consoled. We knew tragedy had struck, but we did not know the source of her pain. Then her husband came out of the four-by-four dwelling in which they lived holding their lifeless child. I was overwhelmed.

She took the baby from her husband and rolled on the ground with her child in her arms. Then she got up and walked in my direction completely overcome by emotion. Though alive, the woman almost appeared more lifeless than the child she was holding. Without hesitation she held out her arms with the baby in her hands.

"Please take her," she insisted.

I could not move.

She pushed the child onto me and fell on the ground again.

My world stopped! The scene was surreal, and my emotions were swirling. In one moment we were wonderfully in the Spirit, rejoicing in new life. The next, I was staring at death and filled with sorrow and grief. I was out of sorts, so someone took the child from me. Some of our women embraced the grieving mother and mourned with her.

The men appropriately left the scene in prayer, yet our hearts were wrenched within us. This was our ministry life in Buchanan. There were many victories and many defeats. There was much joy and much sorrow. Those three years would challenge my faith beyond measure, molding and shaping me into the man God was calling me to be. He would teach me lessons of faith in the strangest of ways, yet I knew it was the only way I could learn.

As I was growing, our church was growing as well. I would preach on Sunday mornings with the goal of raising up one of the young men we were discipling to take the church in a few months. One thing amazing to me about Sunday mornings were the clothes people would wear. We were in the middle of war, and Liberians would dress to the hilt in African attire to come to church. They wore beautiful, handsewn, stylish garments. They also had wonderful Western-world attire and prided themselves on their various forms and fashions.

Andrea, on the other hand, found herself in quite a predicament. Every time she washed her clothes and hung them out to dry, ladies would walk by and steal some of them off the line. They took skirts, blouses and underwear, too. Andrea's selections were becoming limited. She could look in her closet and truly say, "I have nothing to wear."

One particular Sunday, I was teaching from the pulpit. We were now in a slightly larger venue as the Lord was multiplying the church daily. I am sure I was teaching about God's love when a woman walked in wearing one of Andrea's blouses. She actually came to church wearing something she had stolen from my wife! I could not believe it. I was very upset but continued teaching about the love of God. After service, I saw my wife make her way toward the woman.

I was proud of her. Andrea is not very confrontational, so this was a big step for her. I made my way over to the two women and listened intently to how my wife was going to give it to her for stealing the shirt. Andrea gently approached her and gave her a hug.

*She's very calm. I like that,* I thought to myself.

"I have the perfect skirt to match that blouse," Andrea said. "Why don't you come home with me, and I will give it to you."

I could not believe it. *What was she thinking?* This woman needed to know she was wrong. She needed to come to the truth. You cannot reward stealing with blessing or reward. I was going to have to talk to my wife to help her understand that this form of discipleship was not healthy for our growing church.

I was appalled as I watched the woman follow Andrea home and take the skirt. I could not believe what had just transpired.

"Honey, can you please follow me into our room?" I said sweetly. Closing the door, I looked at her and asked, "What were you thinking?"

For about ten minutes I explained how this was not the wisest decision to make. "Think of what you are teaching her," I explained.

Andrea listened quietly. At the end of my monologue, she simply said, "What part of 'when they take your tunic, give them your cloak' do you not understand?"

I was silenced. She was right, and I was wrong.

In fact, the next week the woman gave her heart to the Lord. I was really wrong. We cannot act like the world when the world naturally acts in their folly and sin. We must act like the Lord and win them over with conduct that best represents Him.

This was our life in Buchanan.

# 10

# BEWARE OF DEVOTION TIME

*"Pure and undefiled religion before God and the Father is this: to visit orphans and widows in their trouble, and to keep oneself unspotted from the world."—James 1:27*

*"But whoever keeps His word, truly the love of God is perfected in him. By this we know that we are in Him."—1 John 2:5*

## 1996

Jesus made it very clear at the end of the Sermon on the Mount that "whoever hears these sayings of Mine, and does them, I will liken him to a wise man who built his house on the rock" (Matthew 7:24).

It is important to catch the three words in the middle of this verse: "And does them...." They represent the essence of wisdom. For by it, when the storms of life come our direction, we will know how to apply the knowledge we have gained through the Word in order to be able to stand firm.

Unfortunately, how many times have we neglected those words due to the lack of comfort or convenience within the situation to make the wise decision? I have always been refreshed and rejuvenated by water. Lake or ocean side, staring at the stillness or hearing the roaring surf, always seems to be the place where I can get alone and meet with God. When I find myself engrossed in the demands of daily life, I often go to the water's edge to clearly hear the voice of the Lord.

Andrea and I needed to travel to Monrovia, the capital city, on a monthly basis to get supplies. We loaded up the small car we had with 100-pound bags of rice, sugar and flour to make it through another month of feeding close to thirty people a day. Spiritually, getting away was important as well.

# LIVING PARABLE

During our time in the capital we would stay at a house with missionary friends. Dave and Mary Decker were such a blessing to us. Their home was located right on the beach, and they would always welcome us with open arms and a hot dinner. We looked forward to our time with them because it was a chance for us to unwind, rest, and relax. They had quite a ministry. In fact, they were also our hospital. Any time one of us got sick with malaria or a stomach virus, we found ourselves being nursed to health by Mary's loving and caring touch.

Truly, those weekend experiences became our touch of heaven. I can only imagine how Elisha felt when the Shunammite woman built a small room off the side of her house for the prophet to be able to get away and be with the Lord. Trust me, refreshing the hearts of the saints is a vital ministry for those who are on the front line. If you find you have the opportunity, be a blessing to someone today.

Ministry can be hard. It is easy to get discouraged with so much resting on your shoulders; it can feel like you are holding the weight of the world. I believe this happens because we try to do more than what God has given us and have become disconnected with the Person who enables us. Sometimes this will result in receiving a rebuke from Jesus: "Get back to your first love." I have also experienced this firsthand.

We had chosen to begin a school in Buchanan for all the kids who were not in school and the teachers who were not working. We needed to construct several student desks, so I contracted a local carpenter to make them. I had given him a large 'good faith' deposit to encourage him to work efficiently since we needed the desks in a couple of weeks.

The man did not show up at our facility at the contracted time for our first delivery. We waited for most of the day to no avail. The following day, we waited again and decided that it was time to visit the man at his shop. Upon arrival, I noticed that no desks were being made.

He was not there.

"He's in the bush cutting more wood," one of his workers said.

"When could we expect the delivery?" I asked, and everyone in the shop was suspiciously quiet or had different answers.

# BEWARE OF DEVOTION TIME

We waited for another few days before I visited the shop again and found our carpenter. There were still no desks to be seen.

"Why haven't you built the desks?" I said.

"Someone has stolen the money," he began to explain. "I need another deposit to start making the desks."

I was furious. *Why did he not come to tell me this before?* I thought. We were desperate since school had already started, so I gave him more money to buy wood to build our desks.

That night I met someone from his shop who told me, "He's stolen the money and he's using it to buy more tools for his shop. Do not give him any more money. There will be no desks," he said.

I went to the shop the next morning to see if this was true. There were new tools and no wood. I was enraged. I left shouting at the man and felt like a complete fool for letting him take advantage of me.

My devotions were in 2 Kings, and I was studying the life of Elijah and his servant, Gehazi. If you know the story, God used the great prophet Elijah to heal Naaman, the Syrian, of leprosy. Naaman wanted to repay Elijah for his deed, but Elijah refused payment because he knew this miracle was of the Lord. However, Gehazi, his servant, was greedy and wanted the money. He went behind Elijah's back and ran after Naaman, telling him a story that led to Naaman giving Gehazi the payment Elijah had refused. Elijah caught Gehazi in his sin, and pronounced God's judgment on him—leprosy.

This passage had given me an idea! The next morning, I woke up early and took my missionary friend with me to the house of the carpenter. We got out of the car, and I walked through the winding pathway to his small house. His wife was cooking in the outside kitchen, and he was sitting on a small log beside the fire. In anger, I put my heel in the ground and walked around the house making a circle in the sand. I lifted my hands and began to pray.

I am mortified that I am even telling you this story.

"Oh, God of the heavens and the earth, the righteous Judge who does no wrong and works in miraculous ways, today I come to you with my hands lifted high in surrender. Your servant has been cheated by this man and taken advantage of through his deceit and cunning behavior. I would ask you to show him that You are the true and living God and that the same leprosy that fell on Gehazi, I pray, would fall on him today."

You can begin to see why I am embarrassed to tell you this.

At that point, the wife's father began to walk toward me as his house was directly up the hill from his daughter's. With my hands still lifted high, I pointed at him with my left hand and said, "If you have come to do anything, I will come to your house and pray for you as well."

I was not in a good mood. My friend who was with me was silent. He did not know what he would witness that day, and to be honest, neither did I. Out of the house ran a woman carrying a bed sheet filled with all of her belongings.

She yelled at me, "I only rent here; don't pray for me!" She ran behind me and left the house never to return. I lowered my hands and began to walk away.

The wife came at me with a frying pan. As I heard her getting closer, I turned and looked down at the ground. I said to her, "If you cross this line, a worse thing will come upon you." She stopped at the line and refused to go any further.

My friend and I walked back to the car. Suddenly, he stopped and said, "Can I walk home?"

I looked at him and said, "Get in the car!"

He obeyed. We left. We were silent.

Several weeks later, I was sitting in my room when someone from the house came to get me. He said that there was a woman at the door who wanted to see me. This was a usual occurrence on a Sunday afternoon, so I followed him to the door. When I looked, it was the entire carpenter's family. I opened the screen, and the wife began to cry.

The carpenter looked at me and said, "Please, pray to your God. We have not been well since you left and were afraid to even cross the line to come here. We waited for the line to be washed away by the rain and are asking for your forgiveness."

# BEWARE OF DEVOTION TIME

I let go of the screen door and ran to my room. Quickly, I got on my knees and sincerely lifted my voice, "God, I was kidding. What I am supposed to do?"

I went back to the front door and prayed for the family. Jesus allowed me to lead them to Him, even though I had acted as an unloving agent against them. I was humiliated before the Lord. In my anger, I had warped the purity of the Word of God and misrepresented our loving Savior. I realized that I had let the work of the ministry take me from the person of the ministry and needed to get away to get back on track.

Sitting on the beach one morning, I was reflecting on the events of the previous weeks. I was ashamed and felt completely disqualified for ministry. I had repented, and, at the same time, was in awe of our all-powerful God. I was not afraid of Him but had developed a healthy fear of Him.

I remember that my devotions were in James. I was pondering the following verse: "Pure and undefiled religion before God and the Father is this: to visit orphans and widows in their trouble, and to keep oneself unspotted from the world."

I had become spotted by the world. I had chosen to act in a manner that did not look like Christ, and I asked God to help me be true to His Word above all things.

At that moment, I noticed a friend of ours walking down the beach. She was an older woman and looked very disturbed. She was holding a small boy in her hands and saw me sitting there, so she walked directly to me.

"Oma (as most older ladies are called in Liberia), what's wrong?"

"The child's mother recently died in childbirth while laboring with twins. One of the twins lived and the other died, and she died shortly after due to internal bleeding," she explained.

The boy she was holding appeared to be almost two years old. He had a large stomach and was covered with scabies from head to toe. He was obviously malnourished and in need of care.

# LIVING PARABLE

"I have no way to take care of this child," she said. "I only knew the family because the deceased girl's mother attended my church, and we were in the same tribe."

Immediately the Lord spoke to me, "What did you read today? What did you pray?"

I ignored Him.

He spoke again in that still, small voice, "This is your child. This is your opportunity to hear My Word and do it."

I ignored Him again. This couldn't be the Lord. *It doesn't happen this way,* I reasoned. You don't read a verse, and then a child shows up!

The Oma would not leave, and the Lord would not leave me alone. His voice seemed unnaturally loud, and it was making me uneasy. So, I got up from the beach and walked to the house, as if putting enough distance across the stretch from our favorite place would create a wall that He could not penetrate.

The Oma followed, and the Lord continued to deal with me. Then, in order to relieve the pressure, I turned and said, "We'll take him."

*Wait a second! What did I just say?* Micaiah was only a year old, and I had not even discussed this with my wife. The Oma's face began to gleam as if the sun had come out on a rainy day. She quickly gave the little boy to me and wiped the tears off her face. We walked together to Andrea, and I said to my wife, "This is our new child...I'll explain later."

The little boy went back with her that day. Andrea and I talked and prayed and realized that the Lord had spoken to us. A few weeks later, after some of the formalities were completed, that little boy became our son; and his name is Andrew James.

We were new parents. We had several older boys living in our home, but now we also had another toddler to take care of. Sadly, AJ, as he became known, did not seem to want to be with us. Think of it; he had lost his mother, lived in several homes for several weeks and was now living with people who looked more like ghosts than human beings. He quickly developed a relationship with Micaiah, but was very distant with Andrea and me.

# BEWARE OF DEVOTION TIME

Andrea, quite naturally, went into mother mode with him. Though it was difficult for her relationally in some ways, she did not let that affect how she cared for him. I had to be the disciplinarian at times. This did not help our relationship because I was the first man in his life since he never knew his father. After some time had passed, I remember pulling out my hair and asking the Lord, "Why would this orphaned little boy not love me?" My focus was off, and I needed help. I decided to seek some counsel from my former field supervisor, Glenn Mason. I thought we would need to find another family for AJ as it just did not seem to be working. Glenn had a different opinion.

"Chet, just love him consistently. He will not always be the little boy that rejects you. One day you will be his best friend," he said. That was hard to believe, but I knew he was right.

It did not get any easier. Nevertheless, I trusted the counsel of my friend and decided that I would consistently love AJ no matter how he chose to behave. After all, we love God because He first loved us. I had come to realize that this Scripture is some of the best parenting advice we can receive.

Over twenty years later, that little boy has become one of my best friends. I am not the best of fathers; but I am his, and he is mine. I look back at that moment on the beach and marvel at the grace of God. There, I wanted to quit and give up because of the fool I had become in anger; yet God was about to bless me with one of my greatest gifts in the world. Oh, the grace of God, who can explain it?

One of the wisest things I have ever done in my life came out of one of my greatest failures. I chose to hear the Word of God and do it. Let me encourage you to do the same. His plan for us is good, pleasing, and perfect. Why choose any other way?

# THE LOST BOYS

*"Furthermore, when I came to Troas to preach Christ's gospel, and a door was opened to me by the Lord."–2 Corinthians 2:12*

## 1996

There is one word that describes the effects of war—"loss." People lost their homes, jobs, farms, lifestyles, family members, their ability to go to school and most of all, their innocence. My greatest grievance was the number of children who lost their childhood because of the foolishness of men. They were known as child soldiers— children as young as four years old fighting in a conflict in which they were only promised five U.S. dollars and a pair of Levi's Jeans.

They were deceived, coerced, abandoned and neglected. They were used, beaten, drugged and slaughtered. Years of their lives were taken from them as they were exploited to fight for fortune and fame, not free-dom. They were told not to be afraid, trained by *Rambo* movies and initi-ated into the gang by committing such atrocities as killing their parents, cutting people's limbs off or drinking human blood. They were innocent children turned into killing machines. Something had to be done.

We began to pray for the Lord to open a door that would allow us entrance into their world. Though it was unpredictable and terrifying, Andrea and I could no longer bear the unheard cry of these kids as they died daily in the jungle. The Lord heard our prayer and provided for us in a unique and interesting way.

Located in our town was an unorthodox Catholic priest. His name was Father John; he spoke the African dialect fluently and had incred-ible relationships with his parish.

# LIVING PARABLE

During the heat of the war, he remained behind the walls of the Catholic mission compound. He had been ridiculed for some of his practices, especially those that befriended the rebel forces, but to me, everyone seemed to make judgment calls on a situation of which they were not a part. From his perspective, he made the best decisions he could, depending on the situation presented to him.

We became friends and I would visit him often at the compound for some tea. We would talk about religion, Liberian politics and any other subject that you were not to discuss if you were going to 'win friends and influence people.'

Father John had connections everywhere in the town. You could not name a person he did not know. If he did not know them, he knew who would know them. He cross-pollinated with rebels, peacekeepers, clergy and diplomats. His door was open to anyone, and he relayed a beautiful picture of the love of Christ to me.

He knew of my passion for ministering to child soldiers and my desire to go behind 'enemy lines' to reach them. One day as I came for a visit, he introduced me to a peacekeeping soldier of rank. He was a major in the force, and after some conversation, was willing to allow me to go in with his team to explore the area. God had opened the door for me to travel in enemy territory with six armed soldiers.

The day had come for our travel. A woman from the United Nations, along with other UN officials who were going to 'monitor' the situation on the ground, accompanied me. We climbed into the back of the six-wheeled, all-terrain army vehicle, and piled onto metal bench seats.

*This is classic, God!* I thought, as I sat between two soldiers holding rifles. As we took the turn onto the dusty road leading to the front line, all of my excitement began to hit my stomach, and I was becoming more nervous than intrigued. I thought about leaving Andrea at the house with crying children. The boys wished me success but looked very anxious about the decision I had made. I knew I was called to this but started to doubt as reality hit.

# THE LOST BOYS

The Lord reminded me of Philippians 4:6, which says, "Do not be anxious about anything, but in every situation, by prayer and petition, with thanksgiving, present your requests to God." (NIV) So, I prayed a quiet but heartfelt prayer. "Lord Jesus, I want to return to raise my children and love my wife. I want to continue the work and not die on this fateful day."

*How is it that something I had longed for had now become something I dreaded?* In the back of that vehicle, the more I prayed, the more peace I received. So I prayed without ceasing.

The Lord said, "Press on."

I had accepted this mission without question, and although my spirit was willing, my flesh was weak. I wanted to jump off the vehicle. We came to the last peacekeeping checkpoint. The area between this checkpoint and the next was known as the buffer zone. It was about a mile long, and seemed to be the longest mile of my life.

The day was beautiful. Though there was not a cloud in the sky and the scenery was absolutely stunning, I felt the presence of an evil force not bound by chains.

I shivered momentarily.

The road winded like a snake through the jungle.

We went through small creeks and bounced on the road filled with potholes. Tall trees extended toward the sky like skyscrapers in New York City. The underlying forest consisted of all shades of green, making it truly amazing.

As we rounded a corner, I could see a bar crossing the road ahead. My heart sank to my stomach because I knew we were entering another world in just a matter of moments. When we approached the rebel checkpoint, a young boy, probably the age of ten, came to the gate. He was holding a rifle I did not recognize at first but would come to know intimately in the years ahead as an AK-47. Then another boy joined him, who was no older than the first, holding a similar weapon.

Something happened inside of me. I was no longer afraid. They were children. Yes, they were holding a weapon that could take my life at any given moment, but the Lord removed my fear and filled me with compassion at first sight. It was as if they were playing a game of cowboys and Indians. This could not be serious, but it was reality. The professional soldiers with whom we were traveling gave these children the respect they seemingly deserved. Calling them "sir," I was impressed with their propriety toward these young boys and followed suit when they inspected the back of our vehicle. One of them smiled at me while the other was simply doing his duty. What seemed to be their headquarters was located on the hill above the checkpoint.

There were threatening signs painted on the walls, little boys running around and a babysitter of sorts that was monitoring all of their activity. He was sitting in a chair made of bamboo and was about seventeen or eighteen years old. Nothing seemed to be too serious, but that could quickly change in a matter of seconds.

The moment was uneventful. The children appeared to know we were coming and allowed us to pass without much hindrance. I had imagined something other than what we experienced and was grateful that my thoughts had not come to pass. Though the journey had just begun, my mind was filled with a peace that surpassed understanding, and my heart was broken for these young children.

Our destination was Cestos City, an oversized village that is only called a city because there are a few cement buildings within its border. Situated where the sea meets the Cestos River, it became a bustling community for trade, especially for those that lived across the river. It was located at the end of the road, and the trip would take a little over four hours.

Before the war, farmers and hunters would bring their goods to the market at Cestos to sell or trade. Country rice, various vegetables and coconuts were among the most valuable commodities to exchange for soap, clothes, seasonings, and the basic necessities of life. Red oil, made from the palm kernel of a palm tree, was also a desired item at market and would trade to the highest bidder.

# THE LOST BOYS

We continued on the road to our destination, passing various rebel checkpoints along the way, and our treatment at many mirrored the first. I even found myself becoming comfortable with my new environment. I was fervent in prayer, but more so with power than in fear. As we came to the midpoint of our journey, there was a very long metal bridge ahead that crossed the Timbo River. This waterway divided the counties, and upon landing on the other side, we would be in River Cess County, known for its witchcraft and superstitions.

In fact, it is believed that there is no paved road to this town because a black cobra bit the Caterpillar as it crossed the bridge, and the machine never started again. Most citizens of this county will not swim in the rivers or oceans because they are told that there are little men that live in the water, known as Neejee. It is believed that they pull at your feet and drown you. From JuJu men to "African sign," River Cess has been full of demonic influences for centuries.

Our driver had slowed down long before we reached the checkpoint at the entrance of the bridge. It seemed that he was aware of something as the soldiers began to talk amongst themselves in a Nigerian dialect. Usually when that happens, they are saying something that they do not want you to hear. All of them perked up from their tiresome responsibility and appeared to be more on the alert than before. Once we stopped, I knew exactly why.

This checkpoint was different. There were very few young boys around. The average age of the rebels at this place seemed to be around twenty. They looked mad and were dressed inappropriately with tall boots, tiny shorts and women's wigs on their heads. In one sense, you wanted to laugh; but in the prevailing mood, you knew that it could cost you your life.

The craziest one of them all approached our vehicle brandishing his weapon. He was not wearing a shirt and looked completely strung out on drugs. I saw one of our soldiers put his shooting finger on the trigger. My prayers of power turned quickly to fear. Funny how that happens!

# LIVING PARABLE

He was shouting, threatening and using every four-letter word you could imagine in the most inappropriate of places in sentence structure. It was almost as if he had developed a language of his own for communication. He challenged our soldiers, and they did not move. He poked his gun at the vehicle, pointed the barrel at our tires and did everything he could to invoke some kind of response from the peacekeepers.

Once again, I was impressed with their professionalism. I, on the other hand, was terrified. All of what I thought would happen at the first checkpoint was being realized. I do not know how I would have handled this moment had it been the first one we encountered. With one word or gunshot, this scene could quickly turn bad. The other rebel soldiers that were on the hill above the checkpoint came down like hyenas approaching their prey to go in for the kill.

Sweat formed on the peacekeeper's brow, and I knew this was serious. My senses were heightened, vomiting seemed inevitable and all I could do to keep myself calm was pray. My prayer went something like this, "Jesus, help. Jesus, help now. Jesus, are You listening? Jesus, help now."

In my mind, this was it. We could do nothing. We had driven to disaster and deserved whatever came our way. I am so thankful that Jesus does not think like me. After a twenty-minute tirade, the young man raised his gun for us to pass. That was it! He was all bark. I am not complaining; it is just that when your mind has told you to prepare for death and your life is spared, you can be a bit confused. However, the tension that could have been cut with a knife subsided as we all took a deep breath. Now, I believe God intervened. Then, I was just thankful to get out of there.

My mind began to wonder what the upcoming checkpoints would be like. *Would they get worse? Would they allow us to pass? Would we make it through this day?* My thoughts aligned with the fact that those boys were terrifying and we were defying them. We survived that moment because the power of the Holy Spirit restrained their evil intentions toward us that day. I give God the glory for all the great things He has done.

# THE LOST BOYS

The remaining checkpoints paled in comparison to the experience we had at the bridge. As we got closer and closer to Cestos, I started to think about the road on the way back. *How would we fair? Now that they knew we were here, would they set a trap for us? Would they ambush us? Would they kill us?*

I was lost in anxiety about something that had not yet occurred. Fear can begin to control you if you allow your mind to take you there. Thus, I had to take my thoughts captive and focus on the moment. I purposed to praise God in my heart to get to a place of peace and thank Him for what He had already done. The Lord brought to remembrance the Scripture to cast all my cares upon Him for He cares for me. The Word brought me peace, and I chose to trust in the Lord with all my heart and lean not on my own understanding.

Challenging endeavor, but productive.

Only a mile or so outside of Cestos, the road began to change. The rocky clay soil turned into sand since the town is beachside. Our driver began to pick up speed as the road improved due to the sandy bottom. Suddenly, we came to a screeching halt. There were bones on the road.

We all got out of the vehicle as if to pay respect to the dead. Grandpa Syl and I decided to walk from there. As he hobbled along due to his limp, we slowly came to the main part of town. It was completely abandoned. In fact, there were red deer running out of government buildings. It looked like a scene from an apocalyptic movie. While Cestos is only a one-dirt-road town, the visual of burnt buildings, empty streets, and human bones was frightening.

Grandpa Syl and I walked down to the riverside. Dugout canoes littered the shoreline. Most of them were destroyed, but one or two appeared to be functional. We assumed that they were rebel-owned and used for crossing the river. However, the other side of the river marked the boundary of another rebel faction, and we could not imagine who would want to cross.

# LIVING PARABLE

The river was as magnificent as I remembered. About a mile across, the pristine beauty of such raw nature was everything you hoped to see when watching a National Geographic documentary. Across the water was a small, sandy beach that appeared to be a landing spot. There was a single coconut palm on that beach standing proudly on its own as if in protest to the jungle that lay behind it.

As we walked back to the main road from the river, Grandpa Syl reminisced about the beauty of this place prior to the war. He seemed to be getting emotional as this visual reminded him of all the pain he suffered throughout the war.

"I wonder if I will ever see my wife again," he said almost to himself. They were separated during the war and had not seen each other for almost seven years. He was sure that she was safe in Ivory Coast, but was extremely worried about her well-being.

"I'm not sure if my son is alive," he sighed, and his grief over the hardship caused by the shrewd avarice of a few registered in his voice—and in his face, a rare cameo of pathos.

The devastation was senseless.

I felt his pain.

Just before we reached the main road, we heard a whimper that drew our attention. We were excited to know that somebody was there. We began to walk in the direction of the sound and found a woman crawling out of an abandoned tire shop.

She was battered, and her clothes were ripped. Her hair was a mess and she could hardly walk. She appeared to be dazed and was wiping some blood from her lip. Our pace quickened to get to her aid. I had begun to open the first aid box I carried when she collapsed on the road; we ran to get to her. She was sobbing, and Grandpa Syl began to speak to her in Bassa, the dialect of the area.

"What happened?" He asked her.

"Thirty men raped me all night," she said. One after the other, they stole her dignity and left her for dead. I was holding the reality of war in my hands. Broken and tattered, this precious soul was holding on for dear life, yet seemed to be unsure if she wanted to continue to live.

From a distance, we heard singing. The lady we were holding shot up with an adrenaline rush that I had never seen before. She looked like a deer caught in headlights, and with every ounce of energy she could muster, darted back to the tire shop like a rabbit running to its hole for safety.

Grandpa Syl and I were the only ones on the road. The peacekeeping soldiers and UN workers had decided to go around the area and leave us to wander on our own. The singing got louder, and I realized it was more like chanting. It was not a peaceful sound; in fact, it began to unnerve me. I was beginning to get concerned and wondered what we should do. The lady was no longer in sight, but the oncoming pickup had just come into view. It was filled with about thirty rebel soldiers piled in the back, on the roof, on the side, on the bumper and in the cab. The Liberians appropriately called this type of vehicle a "porcupine pickup" because it looked like a large porcupine with the weapons pointed in the air as they traveled down the road.

There was nowhere to run. Considering his physical limitations, Grandpa Syl would not have made it very far without being seen. In a matter of seconds, we were surrounded. The boys had spotted us and made a beeline in our direction. They slammed on the brakes kicking up dust all around. They jumped out of the pickup and swarmed around us like bees on honey.

There was no time to think. The moment for which I had been waiting had arrived. I was in personal contact with the child soldiers to whom my heart had longed to minister for so long. They were pointing at us, yelling at us, pushing us, and shoving us as if we were part of the dirt on the road. There was no respect for our age, stature or being. They were holding up their guns and shouting in victory, and it reminded me of the lost boys in *Peter Pan*.

They were children.

# LIVING PARABLE

"We are here to help you but refuse to do anything if you continue to treat us like this," I yelled at the top of my voice, shocking myself. They were shocked as well.

Grandpa Syl chimed in and said, "He's right. We can't do anything if you act like this." *What were we going to do?* I thought for a moment. I only had a small first aid kit. There was not enough medicine or bandages to help everyone, and I had just announced that we were going to do something.

Surprisingly, the rebel boys calmed down. All of a sudden, it seemed as if we had control of the situation. There was nothing we had done, nothing we had said and nothing we had performed. We were simply an old man and a young guy holding a first aid box and standing in the middle of the road. We were surrounded by young boys with big guns and completely helpless. Then it hit me, "The heart of the king is in the hand of the Lord." I had read this verse from Proverbs earlier that week.

God had taken control, and I was filled with confidence. Like sheep following a shepherd, the boys followed us to a cement slab next to an abandoned building. Grandpa Syl directed them to stand in line, and we started administering first aid to treat their wounds, providing antibiotics and Ibuprofen. As I cleaned wounds and bandaged rotten sores, they laid their guns down beside my chair while another boy watched me intently.

My tone had become directive. They were only children being led by a few teenagers. They had become more and more respectful with every soldier I helped. The scene is impossible to describe, and I am sure it is difficult to imagine. However, it was my reality at that moment, and I had to make do with what was in front of me. I felt like Moses when he watched the waters of the Red Sea part; all he could do was walk through. God had parted the seas and I was simply walking.

After about thirty minutes of helping the boys, my mind ran to the woman we had seen prior to their arrival, and it hit me—these were the boys who had raped her! At that point, I was faced with a personal dilemma. How could I continue to help the ones who had caused so much pain? My soul wrenched within me. On one hand, I was upset with these children for what they had done; and on the other, I was grieved for these children who needed attention.

I could hear Jesus speak to me almost audibly, "Love your enemy. Pray for, bless and do good to them."

That direction would guide me over the next three years of ministry among these children. Love is the most excellent way, and the only weapon that could end this crisis. Therefore, we gathered the boys and shared the gospel with them as they listened intently. One of the boys interrupted me and showed me his denominational membership card. It was as if he was telling me that this card was his security for salvation. He was not the only child who had one in his pocket; several of them relied on this false hope.

"Jesus is the only way, the truth and the life, and no man can get to the Father except through Him," I said lovingly. While they seemed to agree, no one was willing to make a stand for the gospel. We pressed on for a couple of hours until the peacekeepers returned. There was a formality between them and the child soldiers, and soon the young boys picked up in their vehicle and left. Unfortunately, we never found the lady again. She was no longer in the tire shop, and all we could do was pray for her. We took solace in the hope that quite possibly the Lord used us as a distraction to allow her to get away.

Oh, the great grace of God, who can understand it? It was getting late, and we wanted to get out of rebel territory before nightfall. We all piled into the vehicle, and though the driver pressed the start button several times to ignite the engine, there was not even a spark. One of the soldiers got out and opened the hood and checked a few things.

"Try again," he asked the driver, but nothing happened.

We all got out and took a look under the hood as if we knew what to do. Grandpa Syl had been a mechanic and was the most educated in the group. He tinkered with the fuel line, the fuel filter and the spark plugs, but the vehicle would not start.

# LIVING PARABLE

"I'm going to pray," I said after about an hour of this roadside checkup. One of the soldiers laughed.

"Please join me," I asked everyone as I laid my hands on the hood. The prayer was simple and short. I did not want to stress the situation, but really believed the Lord wanted me to do this.

Almost begrudgingly, the commanding officer said, "Give it a try."

The driver put his hand on the button and it started. There was a huge sigh of relief from everyone, as well as much laughter. We immediately piled in. I praised God silently the whole way home. He had revealed His power in such incredible ways on this trip.

*Lord, I pray for boldness to return and a passion to save the lost,* I prayed silently. *I pray for the woman that we could not find and ask you to please wrap Your loving arms around her. I pray for the soldiers in the vehicle with me. And Lord...here am I, send me.*

# MINISTERING SPIRITS

*"For I was hungry and you gave Me food; I was thirsty and you gave Me drink; I was a stranger and you took Me in."—Matthew 25:35*

*"The Spirit of the Lord is upon Me, Because He has anointed Me to preach the gospel to the poor; He has sent Me to heal the brokenhearted, to proclaim liberty to the captives And recovery of sight to the blind, to set at liberty those who are oppressed."—Luke 4:18*

## 1996

Have you ever been asked by God to do something you did not want to do? Maybe you are unlike me and do not have some of those struggles, but it seems that the Lord is always pushing me to go places or do things that do not fit into my plan, schedule, or personal comfort level. Once again, the Lord was directing me to return to the rebel boys whom I had met on my first journey with the peacekeepers.

"Lord, I've already left my home and moved to Africa," I explained to Him in prayer. "I've left Monrovia and moved to Buchanan to be closer to the rebel boys. I think it would be safer for me to stay in Buchanan and let them come to me."

"It was safer for Me to stay in heaven, yet I gave my life for you," the Lord said to me, and then reminded me of an experience I had as a teenager.

During college, I worked as a lifeguard on Fort Lauderdale Beach. It was one of the best experiences of my life. I enjoyed the men and women who worked alongside me. I was the youngest of the group, and they treated me like a younger brother by taking care of and making fun of me.

# LIVING PARABLE

One night, I was with a friend of mine and we decided to go and share the gospel on the streets at the beach. While we were there, the Lord spoke to me.

"Walk toward your usual lifeguarding tower," He said.

My friend and I began to head in that direction, when we saw that a young man was sitting at the base of my tower. I figured it was for him that the Lord had sent us in that direction and began to share with him the love of Jesus. He listened politely as he played his guitar and then said, "You Christians always come and share the gospel with us, but I am hungry and have nowhere to sleep. Why don't you take me home and feed me?"

My evangelism course had not trained me for that. I was about nineteen years old at the time and was living at home with my parents.

What would they think? I began to use that as an excuse in my mind and reasoned with the young man. He understood, but the Lord was not finished with me.

"Take him home," the Lord said to me. Although I wrestled with the practicalities of this thought, it ended with him following me to my car as I agreed to take him to my house. On our way to the car, two of his friends stopped us.

"Hey, this guy is a Christian," the young man said to them. "I am going to his house tonight. Why don't you come?"

I thought it best to interrupt him, but the boys had already agreed to come over, and now the four of us were making our way to my car. On the drive home, we talked about everything from politics to religion. I was nervous about what my parents would say, but I figured that if they refused, it would be my excuse to take them back to the beach.

When we got home, my parents were already in bed. I informed them of the situation and my mom got out of bed. Without saying much, she took some spaghetti out of the fridge, heated it up, set some plates out and went back to bed. She simply served.

"Wow!" The boys were amazed. They could not believe that my mom did not kick them out. After she had left, they wanted to hear more about Jesus. I had tried convincing them all night, but this simple act of feeding them spaghetti was the turning point for their openness to hearing the gospel. It was late by the time they finished eating, so they went to sleep on the couch. I prayed through the night for protection!

Early the next morning, I dropped them off at the beach. I had given them some clean socks and clothes, as they did not have much. We talked about the evening on the way, and they were grateful for all we had done. However, one of them did not speak much. He was silent the whole time we were together. I wondered what his story was, but did not push and simply hoped that we had planted some seeds of the gospel.

That afternoon I went to the locker room after working on the beach. After opening the combination lock to my locker, I found the pair of socks and clothes I had given the young boys neatly folded inside, and the Lord reminded me of Hebrews 13: "You will entertain angels...."

This incident affected the way I approached God's direction for my life. Samuel told Saul that "obedience is better than sacrifice," yet my struggle is to be sure that it is the voice of the Lord and not the voice of Chet. Therefore, I have always sought confirmation through His Word, prayer and wise counsel. Thus, everything pointed toward going "behind the lines" to minister to child soldiers.

"I agree," said Andrea, and so we began to pray through the plan. Though our spirit wanted to obey, our flesh was very weak.

Jim Elliot has always been a hero of faith for me. His wife's book, *Through Gates of Splendor*, inspired me in my journey because to quote Jim Elliot, "He is no fool who would choose to give the things he cannot keep, to find what he can never lose."

As Elizabeth Elliot writes the story, her husband and four other men gave their lives for the gospel on a beach one day, purposing to minister to the Auca Indians in Ecuador.

"Lord, I hope I have that kind of faith and to be that kind of man—willing to lay my life down in the same manner," I prayed, purposing to read that book like a manual.

# LIVING PARABLE

His journal entries, which were included in the book, his approach to ministry and manner of life became my direction. We planned our trip in the same way he had planned his, yet hoped the ending would be different. My wife had always asked the Lord for a man like Jim Elliot, but as the trip approached, we began to realize the cost involved and had many conversations to encourage each other to press on.

With the money we had saved, I purchased everything from soccer balls to slippers as gifts for the boys. We made 'love bags' of soap, salt, seasonings, rice, oil and beans to give anyone we encountered on the road—much like my mom making spaghetti for those boys that night at my house.

The church packaged them all in individual bags and stuffed them into old rice bags to take with us on our journey. We stored everything at the church and held a prayer session for the trip, our safety, and for God's favor to be upon us.

Andrea and I prayed at home together in the evenings. Our prayers were much more transparent than the "powerful prayers" we prayed at church.

"Lord, I pray for survival and not to be hurt. Jesus, give me the strength not to deny You if they chose to torture me in the way for which they are known." And as an afterthought, I prayed, "For one bullet to the head if it is my time."

Andrea prayed for peace and comfort to make it through the next couple of days of my travels. These prayers were sincere. They were real, and we were desperate for God. The night before our trip, several men tried to break into our home. Unbeknownst to us, on that same night, this same group of men broke into the church and stole all of the bags we had prepared to take on the journey. When they came to our house, they called out to us and said, "Chet Lowe! We hear you can fight. Come on out and fight us."

I felt like I was Nehemiah, and they were Sanballat and Tobiah taunting me to destroy my life.

"Oh, Lord, You know we are Your servants," I yelled back. "These men have come to hurt our lives. Please show them that You are God and consider having their extremities drop off in the process!"

"What kind of missionary are you?" They screamed back.

"I'm a different kind of missionary!" I screamed back.

I know what you may be thinking. I praise God He has not given up on me yet either. This was our life. We had conversations through the bars of our windows with the men that wanted to break into our home and kill us. Thankfully, they left, but it did not provide much comfort to Andrea since I was leaving the next day. That morning, the young men who had slept at the church came running to the house. They explained to us how the men broke in while they were sleeping. They were awakened and threatened with weapons, so they let them take anything they wanted.

The boys were scared. We thanked the Lord that no one was hurt but were saddened our trip would have to be delayed and that all of our supplies were gone. We relayed the message to the church. The Liberian "satellite of communication" is ten times faster than AT&T and Verizon combined. People came to the house to encourage and remind us that God's timing is perfect. I was disappointed because we did not have enough money to repurchase the gifts and knew the trip would have to be further delayed. I really believed God had spoken to me and was wondering how all of this was going to work out.

I even started to doubt. A few days later, I was still dismayed. As I walked to church that Sunday, I continued to consider all that was before us and kept it in prayer. Church started at 10:00 a.m. This allowed everyone to get his or her morning chores done but keep the service in the cool of the day. As people started coming, everyone was holding bags in their hand walking up the road. I had not noticed it at first, but it became very apparent as bags began to pile up at the front door.

They brought slippers, seasonings, oil, rice and clothes. These people were like the widow who gave the only thing she had for the sake of the Lord. Most of our church lived in the displacement center, were out of jobs, or had everything taken from them in the war. They were not giving out of their abundance, they were giving from their hearts. By the end of service, we had enough things to fill even more bags than what we had originally packed. God had used His people to do His work for His glory.

The trip was back on. Our plan was to go all the way to Pillar of Fire mission. This was the compound where I had stayed when I was fourteen years old. We would travel the dirt road to Cestos for four hours, and then take a dugout canoe from the river's mouth into the ocean. We would sail up the coast to Pillar of Fire by way of the sea, as I did not feel it safe to walk through rebel territory.

Pillar of Fire was a safe location, relatively speaking. Even though I had not been there for ten years, I felt like I knew the area. Most importantly, we had heard that the rebel commander there was somewhat friendly. Our plan was to avoid locations where the notorious rebels were known to be. Once we had discovered who the commander was, we asked his father, who was living in Buchanan at the time, to consider going with us on the trip to speak to his son on our behalf. Everything seemed as if it was going according to plan, and God's favor was upon us each step of the way.

The night before our trip, I reflected on how the Lord had orchestrated all of the events so that no man could receive credit because of how He had provided. Originally, I did not want to go on this trip and was very hesitant to obey the voice of the Lord.

Now, there was nothing but excitement in my heart and great expectation. He had taught me much earlier in my life to trust His direction, and now, I was staring at bags of supplies in as much awe as when I had opened my locker.

# MINISTRY MONKEYS

*"But we, brethren, having been taken away from you for a short time in presence, not in heart, endeavored more eagerly to see your face with great desire."*
*—1 Thessalonians 2:17*

*For I long to see you, that I may impart to you some spiritual gift, so that you may be established."—Romans 1:11*

## 1996

The morning of the trip had come. Grandpa Syl arrived early as we were packing the car. Johnny, the only Liberian willing to go with me, was strapping bags on the roof and helping me stuff the car with twelve bags of goods. Johnny had recently come to know the Lord while we were living in Monrovia. He was dating a very good friend of Andrea's, and we were able to lead him to the Lord through their relationship.

Johnny was a fellow soldier and, better yet, a faithful friend. He was witty, brave, and courageous, and he called me "big brother." He had an incredible street smart about him, so I was glad he was going on the trip with me. From the moment he committed his life to the Lord, he was willing to surrender all.

Grandpa Syl, Johnny, the rebel commander's father and I stuffed ourselves into a four-door Toyota hatchback. We referred to this vehicle as the 'mobile' because like the army mobiles that went anywhere, this vehicle had taken us all over the place. Besides, its muffler had a hole in it that caused it to sound like a freight train instead of a car. With all four of us plus our twelve bags in the car, we prayed and pulled away from our house to start the journey.

# LIVING PARABLE

We looked ridiculous with bags all over the place, but this was normal in Liberia. Vehicles were limited because of the war, and anything that moved could be used for anything you needed. We also put two spare tires on the roof to prepare for anything that might happen. That day we needed Batman's Batmobile, which is designed to go fast, and it's armed with cannons and other crazy weaponry, but more importantly, it can transform into a tank!

Everyone sitting in that car knew the journey ahead was going to be difficult. In fact, when we got to the last peacekeeping checkpoint before the buffer zone, we asked ourselves if we were really going to move forward. There were no soldiers with us this time, and it had rained the night before. I am sure I do not have to explain what rain does to a dirt road, but in the event you have never been out of the city, it turns to mud.

The car was loaded down, and the frame continued to hit the dirt with every pothole we crossed. Grandpa Syl, our driver, would have to take the road very slowly and purpose to avoid as many holes as he could. The shocks on the vehicle were not good, but it was all we had to conquer these jungle roads; so we pressed on.

I began to think of the checkpoint at Timbo River. I was concerned about crossing due to the crazy young man we had met there before. My mind had wondered, and I was brought back to reality when I noticed that water was seeping into the vehicle due to the crater in which we were stuck. One rule you should always follow while driving in the jungle is, "Follow the fresh tracks." Since we were the ones making the tracks, Grandpa Syl drove right into this hole thinking he could make it through.

We did not.

We were stuck in the mud.

Without hesitation, we took all of the bags out of the car and off the roof to lighten our load. The car was sinking, and we did not want the engine to go under water and flood. As quickly as we could, we tromped through the mud, trying not to sink, as we pushed the vehicle out of the hole.

Nothing was working.

The car was not moving.

# MINISTRY MONKEYS

Thankfully, we had stopped at a small village. In a few minutes, many of the people had gathered to watch the white man and his friends. It must have been sheer entertainment seeing our performance. We were falling in mud. We were covered in mud, and digging through it. When they had seen enough, they decided to come and help. It was at that point I realized why we had this little car. The village men helped us pick up that small vehicle and push it to freedom. As we repacked our little mobile, I looked at that dilapidated car a little differently and was grateful for God's provision.

Checkpoint after checkpoint, we had to take down all the bags and reload them. I satisfied the rebel boys by giving them a soccer ball and was grateful for Jim Elliot's example of dropping gifts as a means to create relationship. The soccer ball was a huge success on many fronts. It created such excitement that the boys forgot about the other bags, and during all of the commotion, we slipped unhindered through each checkpoint after reloading the bags.

By God's grace, the soccer plan even worked with the crazy man at Timbo River. He came at us in full force as he did the first time. Once again, he was dressed in shorts, tall boots, no shirt and a woman's wig. I was beginning to think that he thought this was his uniform. As soon as he approached the car, I stuck my hand out of the window waving a soccer ball. I think it was pure survival instinct on my part, but in any case, we did not even have to take down all of the bags to pass through. Finally, we made it to Cestos with all of our goods. I want to point out that this was a miracle. We had passed over ten checkpoints along the way and did not lose one bag or any of its contents. Rebels were notorious for taking people's belongings as they traveled, but God had answered our prayer and delivered us from the evil ones.

When we arrived, there were people in the town. It had been a couple of months since our last visit, and apparently, things had settled. We drove down to the waterside and hoped to find a group that would be willing to carry us in a dugout canoe to Pillar of Fire.

# LIVING PARABLE

Several people gathered to listen to the negotiations of our deal, as this was one of the biggest events that had happened in the town for quite some time. Once we had negotiated the price with our person, we started loading the bags on the canoe. The canoes were dug out of large trees, making them porous, which means they leaked, and were extremely unstable. Once we loaded our canoe and got inside, the rim was only about two to three inches above the waterline. We realized we needed to lighten our load.

We gave some of the bags to Grandpa Syl to distribute in Cestos. This proved to be a good idea in the long run. Those that were standing by the river were upset that we had not given them anything. God allowed our overloaded canoe to correct our mistake.

Since we now had about four inches above the water line, we felt safer for some reason. We cast off the shoreline and headed for the river mouth that dumped into the ocean. Johnny, the father of the rebel commander, and I were in the canoe with two other Liberians sailing our "ship." Grandpa Syl remained behind, and the look of concern on his face penetrated my soul.

We paddled gently down the river. Our responsibility was to bail out the water seeping in while the two Liberian sailors diligently kept us moving forward. We rounded a turn and saw the ocean. There was only one problem. Between the ocean blue and us was a series of swells that appeared to be four to five feet tall.

The Liberian sailors assured us that they would go between the sets of waves, and we would be fine. When I looked at Johnny, who had just told me that he could not swim, I saw terror for the first time on his face.

We approached the first swell very carefully. Then, when the sailors thought the time had come, they paddled profusely to pick up momentum and get out into the ocean before the next round. As a surfer, I was impressed with their timing, and it seemed that we were on track for an uneventful course through the waterway.

This hope was quickly dashed. On the horizon, I saw a large swell approaching the canoe. The sailors saw it as well and began to paddle like madmen. I looked behind me, and Johnny's eyes were as big as saucers. By God's grace, we made it over the top of the swell and the relief in my heart was overwhelming. However, we were not out of the woods just yet. Our timing was off and there was another swell on the way. I could tell the sailors were getting tired as the canoe was beginning to slow down. The wall of water approaching us was getting bigger and bigger. It was going to break; there was no way around it. Our canoe would have to go through this wave or be consumed by it. The sailors faced the wave head on. The wave broke directly in front of us, and a wall of white water was headed our way.

"Hold on!" I screamed to Johnny, as the water hit us in the face and began filling the canoe.

"Bail the water! Bail the water! Bail the water!" The sailors screamed at us, as they paddled with all their might. We followed in like manner and bailed and bailed, and bailed the water.

I looked up and saw another swell. If we took in more water, I could not see the canoe staying afloat.

"Paddle!" I screamed to the sailors to somehow encourage their weary bodies to press on. As if in slow motion, the swell approached us, and we were at its mercy.

I whispered, "Oh, God!"

Only by His control did the swell roll right under us and crash into the stern of the canoe. The horizon looked clear, the sailors paddled, we bailed, and we made it to the ocean blue.

The sun was setting as the sail made of old rice bags sewn together was being hoisted. The shoreline was lined with golden sand and coconut trees that stretched out for miles on end. The ocean's swells that once terrified us were now lulling most of the travelers to sleep. Crunched in the canoe, I tried to absorb every view of this incredible sight as the sun went down on the horizon.

# LIVING PARABLE

Several hours later, I was awakened. It was very dark. I could hear the ocean waves crashing on the beach, but I could only see one small light that shined like the North Star in the midst of the dark night. We were only about two hundred yards from shore.

"Permission to land!" The sailors called out at someone on the beach.

"Sleep on the ocean!" A voice answered back. After our experience coming out to sea, this was unacceptable to all of us on board.

"We are coming ashore!" We yelled back, and the sailors approached the shore with caution. It was night, and the light someone was holding on the beach was our only guide. We could hear the waves but were not sure where they were forming or breaking.

Unfortunately, they knew where we were. In one motion, our canoe was thrown, and I was toppled into the sea. By God's grace, one of the sailors and I were the only ones thrown. We swam to shore as Johnny held onto the canoe for dear life. When I reached the beach, the canoe was thrown by the shore break, and everyone toppled onto the shoreline. All of our bags were thrown as well, and we quickly tried to secure the canoe on the beach. Once the canoe was clear, I sat down on the sand in utter exhaustion. Yet, something did not feel right. More than a physical injury, I sensed uneasiness in my spirit.

Instinctively, I turned my neck around to see if someone was behind me. When I looked, there were six young boys holding machine guns to my head. There was no time for my life to flash before me. The only thing I thought of was my family. Looking down the barrel of those weapons was terrifying. My life was in their hands, but truly, I had already placed my life in the palm of the Lord.

The Word says, "No weapon formed against us shall stand" (Isaiah 54:17). At that moment, I felt as if that had been written just for me.

"Get up," one of the boys said, and in that instant, I was relieved. For some reason, I felt that my life was spared with that command. Then, just as the lost boys carried Wendy to Peter Pan, these six- and seven-year-old children carried me to their leader.

"We have brought your commander's father with us," I said as we walked.

"How's Leo doing?" I asked as if I knew him personally. The little boy turned around and laughed.

"Leo was moved last week, Albert is here," he said, laughing.

The very name shrieked terror in my being. Albert was known as a dreaded warrior. We had purposed to avoid any area in which he was located, and now, he was in charge of my life. I took every step in fear with prayer, begging God to spare me. Johnny and I were thrown into a courtyard of sorts. Makeshift oil lamps illuminated the night. They had cut ropes to be used as wicks and laid them on a plate of red oil. There was an eighteen-year-old boy sitting in a bamboo chair behind a table, with two younger boys fanning him with palm branches.

"Hello," I said, but he did not speak to me.

This was bad.

He looked at the young boys that were holding us there with their guns on our backs and motioned to them swiping his hand across his neck. I believe this is the international sign for slice their throat. I have used it with my kids to tell them to be quiet, but I do not think that was his intention. The boys began to move and gestured for us to move with them.

My feet were stuck. I could not move. I could not speak. I was just there. The whole world seemed to close in on me, and Johnny nudged me to move. Right then, young children came screaming up the path. It startled me back to reality, as I watched them throw our bags in front of Albert like pirates would to the captain of their ship.

Pulling and pushing, they ripped at the bags like carnivorous sharks in a frenzy over dead fish. The scene was getting out of control until Albert stood up. At this, everyone quieted. He looked at us and pointed toward a small hut next to where he was sitting. The boys took us there and locked us in what seemed to be a bedroom.

# LIVING PARABLE

There was dancing and shouting. The boys were singing and parading around, holding all of the goods that we had brought. I looked through a slat in the wall and saw one of them pretending to take a bath with a bar of soap that was still in the package. Then, they lit a fire and started dancing around it. I had heard that the rebels were cannibals. I looked at Johnny and said, "They are going to eat us." I was not kidding!

We stayed awake all night and so did the boys. It seemed that they would never settle from their excitement and appeared to be nocturnal. Thankfully, by the early hours of the morning, the place calmed, and we were able to rest. We were exhausted and sleep came quickly. I am not sure how long we slept, but someone opening the door eventually awakened us. We were asked to come outside, and we followed instruction. Still groggy from sleep, my eyes were adjusting to the light as we walked into the courtyard.

Albert was sitting in his seat and said, "Morning."

His demeanor had changed. It appeared as if he was being friendly and wanted to make conversation.

"Good morning," I said.

"What are you doing here?"

"I am a missionary and God has sent me to you. Jesus loves you enough to send me all the way from the United States to tell you that you are loved."

Spirituality, it seemed to be the only thing that mattered at that point for I did not know what this day would hold. Albert listened intently. He was a handsome young man. He was very dark, in fact, almost purple. His hair was styled, and he was wearing fashionable clothes, which made him look like an American high school football player.

"Follow me," he said as he got up, and Johnny and I obliged.

We walked around the mission. I felt at home. We saw the church, the school our team had built and the mission house I had slept in when I got malaria. Of course, it was all destroyed or damaged during the war, but the Lord had brought me back in one piece.

# MINISTRY MONKEYS

Albert spoke of his exploits in the war.

"I am a liberator; I am a hero," he said.

Johnny and I simply nodded our heads and listened to everything he had to say. In some strange way, it felt like he was becoming our friend. I was not sure if this was some kind of tactic to get information out of us or not, but my only concern at that moment was that we were alive.

He allowed us to tell him more about our mission.

"Could I operate a clinic for the civilians?" I said.

"Yes, as long as you treat the soldiers as well," he said, and I agreed. By that afternoon, I had everything set up and started seeing people one by one. Most of the 'patients' suffered from cuts and abrasions, stomach ailments and infections. The child soldiers had bullet wounds, machete cuts and sexually transmitted diseases. Two boys came into my office with bullet wounds on their extremities. Fragments were embedded in the foot of one and the hand of another.

"How did you get these?" I asked.

"We were playing a game," the boys said in unison, as they explained their deadly game. They took ten paces, turned and fired.

"How were you trained?"

"Rambo!" They screamed.

*Who says that movies do not affect our youth?* I thought.

Every story was connected to a tragedy. For the rest of the afternoon and most of the next day, I treated individuals as best as I could, praying with them and sharing the gospel. The Lord had opened a door, and I was purposed to walk through it.

People who are in need of care, whether friend or foe, are always willing to listen to the one who is offering the helping hand. This was the manner of Jesus. He sent the disciples to do good and preach the Word (Matthew 4:23, 9:35; Luke 9:6). The two go hand in hand. One cannot go on without the other if it is in Jesus' name.

On the afternoon of the third day, it was time to leave. We had decided the footpath was safer at this point because the sea had not treated us so well. Albert sent soldiers with us for safekeeping.

# LIVING PARABLE

"Can we come back?" He expressed his consent by giving us a monkey, and we were on our way. After three hours of walking and crossing the Cestos, Grandpa Syl was waiting for us on the shoreline of the river in absolute relief. We loaded the vehicle, monkey and all, and started our journey home. Little did we realize a new adventure was yet before us.

# 14

## KNOCKED OUT BY GOD

*"From whom the whole body, joined and knit together by what every joint supplies, according to the effective working by which every part does its share, causes growth of the body for the edifying of itself in love."*—Ephesians 4:16

### 1996

If you have ever been an athlete or competed in any way, you know that coaches have a way of pushing you beyond what you think you can bear. Their purpose is to train you and help you reach your highest potential. Oftentimes, the athlete may see it as cruel and unusual punishment if his perspective has been taken off the goal. However, if the focus of victory remains, it is amazing what the athlete will endure in order to win.

Paul tells us in 1 Corinthians 10 that the Lord will not give us more than we can handle. He constantly uses a sports comparison to challenge the believer to be "a strong athlete," "run in such a way as to win the prize," and "exercise yourself toward godliness."

I believe this metaphor is being used by the Holy Spirit to spur us on toward love and good works. However, we need to keep in mind that He is our coach. In that, the writer of Hebrews reminds us that sometimes we need a spur in order to move forward. A spur is a reminder to the horse that the cowboy is in control. A tap with the spur on its side compels the horse to follow the rider's direction.

The same is true of sports. The coach is there to get the athlete to victory. His purpose is to help the competitor go beyond himself by providing the accountability to press on and the knowledge of how to actually win. As the coach works with the athlete, both will achieve victory though only one runs to compete for the prize.

# LIVING PARABLE

In my years of training, very rarely did I choose my workout. My coach knew exactly what I needed to get better, and my involvement in the plan was obedience, never input. Likewise, I realized very quickly on our way home from Cestos that God's plan and mine were drastically different. After several days of grueling ministry, I wanted to sleep in the back of our Toyota hatchback.

But the Lord said, "I am not finished with the workout yet."

Johnny and I were exhausted from the trip. My feet were on fire with broken blisters on the top and bottom from the seven-mile walk. Gradually I realized that my sandals had been rubbing dirt between the strap and my flesh. Liberians wear flip-flops on their treks through the jungle due to the many streams that need to be crossed. I wanted to be like them in everything and decided to do the same. In one sense, it was good as it prevents you from getting jungle rot on your feet. On the other hand, my feet were not used to this form of travel yet and had some toughening up to do.

We had left the commander's father in the jungle. He wanted to stay a few extra days to gather coconuts to sell in Buchanan. With one less traveler and no more bags, I had the entire back seat to myself. The sun was going down, and black clouds were forming, which provided a wonderful coolness in the air that was lulling me to sleep. Of course, there were the occasional potholes that caused me to hit my head on the metal of the car every once in a while, but the in-between snoozes were well worth the disturbance.

Grandpa Syl was doing his best to make it home before it got too late. Night caught us in the bush behind enemy lines. The sense of darkness was both physical and spiritual. We had passed several checkpoints unhindered, but we still did not feel safe in that neck of the woods.

The dark clouds that had formed prior to the sun setting began to release their torrential rains. We could not see through the windshield due to the sheets of water that covered our car. The road began to look like a flowing river, and the potholes were being covered so that we could not see how to maneuver successfully to avoid them. Our pace slowed to that of a snail, and our hope was that the rain would not cause the river to overflow and cut the road abandoning us on the wrong side of this dark place. Our little mobile labored intensely through those jungle roads. At times, we needed to help it and got soaking wet while pushing the car in the pouring rain. My feet were caked with red mud, and I knew that if I did not attend to those sores, they would become tropical ulcers in the next few days.

The restful trip I wanted had turned into another nightmare. Thankfully, the rain subsided. It was very late, and we were very tired. Grandpa Syl picked up his speed significantly. I could tell he was nervous and was taking greater risks with speed than previously.

Pow! Pow!

I thought we had been shot. In some sense, we were all expecting something of that nature. Fortunately, it was just our tires. We got out of the car and saw that we had two flat tires. We had brought two spares with us, but one of them had already been used on the first part of the trip. We untied the tires from the roof as Johnny began to raise the front of the car with a jack. Unsure of what we would do for the second tire, we all simply followed suit as if there was a plan in action.

After the first tire had been changed, we began to raise the back of the car to change the second. Grandpa Syl inspected the tire and saw that it had nails in it. He suspected foul play but did not say anything so that we would not worry. Then, we heard something.

Looking behind the car into the night, we saw a man approaching us. He had a machete in his hand and swiped it on the ground. Everything was happening so quickly that I did not have a chance to think. Grandpa Syl and Johnny went to the rear of the car, and I followed them. The man who came toward us was about twenty-five years old. He was definitely a rebel soldier but did not have a rifle in his hand. He approached us and raised the machete in the air.

"Who are you?" Grandpa Syl asked him.

"I am greater than God," he responded with a guttural sound.

"This is my country," said Grandpa Syl infuriated. "These are my people. In fact, this is my land. If you want to spill my blood, you are welcome, but you are *not* greater than God."

This dialogue was not going well.

As I listened to Grandpa Syl's speech, he was confident and secure. I, on the other hand, was thinking: *This is not my country. These are not my people, and this is not my land.*

I thought there was a more diplomatic way to handle this. Even the Word says, "A gentle answer turns away wrath" (Proverbs 15:1 NIV).

I bent down to pick up the tire iron we were using to defend myself. When I came up, my head hit the hatch of the vehicle, and I passed out. It was as if God was saying, "Stay down, Son. I've got this." When I recovered, it was hot and dark. I was concerned for a moment that all hope for me had been lost. As my vision cleared, I saw Johnny and Grandpa Syl sitting on the road attending to me. I jumped, and Johnny grabbed me.

"What happened?" I asked.

"We don't know," Grandpa Syl said. "They came on us. They ran away from us."

We sat there for a moment in silence.

The moment passed and Grandpa Syl was the first to get up. He started stuffing the flat tire with grass and dirt, and Johnny and I looked at each other and quickly helped him. We were unsure of what this would do, but we knew we needed to do something to get out. Placing the dirt-filled tire on the vehicle, we made our way out of that dark night. Every inch was a thump. We were basically on the rim of the back tire, which made for quite a bumpy ride. Even the monkey that we had been given looked at me as if it was disturbed by the mode of transportation to which we had subjected it.

We finally arrived at the buffer zone checkpoint at about 2 a.m. A female soldier approached our car and began to question us. She obviously had something to prove as she pummeled us with questions and accusations. She was so loud and obnoxious that one of the men from the house approached our vehicle as well. As he approached, she screamed across the road that we had aided and abetted the enemy by taking supplies across the river. She was right in saying that we went to their enemy since the faction across the river was a different warring faction than the rebels at our present location. He seemed much more sublime and tried to calm her down. She was insisting that we were the reason this war was continuing and should be tried. The man who came to her call put his arm around her and said, "Baby, let these people go." At that point, she lifted the gate but refused to let us pass as she continued to hurl insults and accusations our way.

Then, another man came out of the house across the street yelling, "Baby! Who are you calling, Baby?" The second man approached the first as if he was getting ready to fight. The two began to brawl over whose girlfriend she was, and the scene became quite entertaining.

"Get back in the car," Grandpa Syl whispered to me.

"But I'm enjoying the show," I whispered back.

He strongly nudged me to obey. So, we got in the car, and he slowly drove away. I could not help myself and looked at the woman and said, "Looks like you caused the war tonight!"

I do not know why, but it felt good.

We rolled loudly through town around three in the morning. The rim was worn, and the muffler had finally broken. We parked at my home, and I walked around to the front door to see if anyone had awakened. No one was moving, so I ran to our bedroom window to see if I could wake Andrea. A candle was lit in the room and was shining out into the dark night. As I looked through the window, there was my wife on her knees whispering, "Lord, please protect my husband."

I wept.

Staring at my beautiful bride on her knees was one of the most incredible sights I had ever seen in my life. In my exhaustion, all I had thought about was how to get through the night in my own strength. I was down, and she was lifting me up. I had not prayed or sought the Lord for His mighty hand of protection. My wife had not left the room much while I was away, and everything clicked at that moment as to our safety.

Prayer is the work of the ministry. Like Moses, my wife knew that she could not go into the battle, but knew she could pray. And like Joshua, I was focused on fighting the enemy. I did not make time for prayer. Yet, the Lord heard my wife as He heard Moses and delivered me from every evil attack. That night I learned that our victory is found in prayer, and we cannot forsake it for the battle. My heavenly coach knew I needed this lesson. I thought it was about enduring. He was pushing me to prayer!

# THIS MEANS WAR

*"For I am not ashamed of the gospel of Christ, for it is the power of God to salvation for everyone who believes, for the Jew first and also for the Greek. For in it the righteousness of God is revealed from faith to faith; as it is written, 'The just shall live by faith.'"*—Romans 1:16-17

## 1996

I was alone and afraid. Both of the Liberian men that were crouching in the forest with me had taken off. Our car had broken down in rebel territory, and we heard another car coming up the road. It sounded as if it was fully loaded with rebel children chanting their familiar songs, so we forsook the car on the road and headed to the bush.

One never knew the mood of the rebels. They could be friendly because of a major victory, or they could be frustrated due to defeat. The best thing to do was to take cover and hope they would simply pass you by. In this instance, that is exactly what we did.

It was night, and the road had become very familiar to us. By this time, we were making monthly trips behind rebel lines, so we were recognized by most of the rebel boys at the checkpoints. In sincerity, the Lord had removed fear from our hearts as we developed these relationships, but there was still the unforeseen, and we had learned to walk in wisdom after making many mistakes. As we squatted in the bush under some branches, one of the Liberian guys took off in another direction.

Then, the other fled as well.

"Where are you going?" I asked him before he ran away.

"With this moon shining, you are glowing like a ghost," he said, and without needing to hear any more explanations, I quickly rubbed dirt on my face and arms and hoped to become invisible to the passing vehicle. Thankfully, the pickup passed and we came out of hiding.

# LIVING PARABLE

"Hey friends, thanks a lot for deserting me..." I said jokingly. We grabbed a pineapple and bananas that were growing nearby and sat on the road eating and laughing.

Not all of our trips involved such drama, but each one of them was an adventure. All of life is a journey. I have heard it said, "The days are long, but the years are short." If you stop and think for a moment of the truth in that statement, you just might follow Scripture and take life from faith to faith, glory to glory or precept upon precept. In other words, choose to enjoy life from the perspective of taking one step at a time.

Jesus made it clear that offenses are going to come. He even said, "In this world you will have tribulation but be of good cheer, I have overcome the world" (John 16:33).

Life has its 'ups and downs.' Most of the time, it happens when we do not expect it. How we walk through this journey is our choice. We can look at life from the context of 'half full' or 'half empty.' The key is to ask the Lord to give you spiritual eyes and ears so that you might see and hear why He has placed you on the journey for His glory.

We looked forward to packing the car and traveling to Pillar of Fire. Albert, the rebel commander of our area, had also given us freedom to travel anywhere in his region as long as we helped both soldier and civilian. We walked for miles, covering two counties in Liberia. We went to any area where there were people. With first aid supplies, small relief items and our Bibles, people always received us with open arms. Well, most all of them.

In many of the areas we traveled, I was the first white man that some of the children had ever seen. *Hwipo-gaa*, which means "white man" in Bassa, had become my name. You could hear children screaming this term in terror as I entered a town. Some would show signs of bravery, but I used the opportunity to put up my hands and fingers and crouch down and yell to play the familiar "run from the scary white man" game.

By the end of my stay, we were all friends. I remember one trip in which we walked the furthest we ever had into the jungle. I prayed, in jest, as we went in, "God, I'm not sure You have ever been here before.

Please, go with me now." I was concerned about this trip and decided to take a few more people with us. For sheer protection, I took one of the guys with me who was six foot two. He had set up a gym at his house and used a car axle for a bench press, as well as other various heavy objects to work out. It was obvious that he spent a lot of time at his improvised gym and had the appearance of a personal bodyguard. My thought was that rebels respected stature. In my mind, he had the image of Goliath, and this was good enough for me.

After taking a canoe up river for an hour, we still had a three-hour walk to the small town. We were greeted with much joy. They used one of the mud structures as a community hall and officially welcomed us to their home. We enjoyed great food and fellowship throughout the night. Later that evening, it was time to retire, and we were each given our own room.

The houses in the interior are made of sticks, mud and palm thatches. They have a very 'open air' feel. As you lay down, you cannot help but stare at the palm thatches intricately woven together, which are stronger than most western-made roofing materials. The noise that fills the night as the jungle comes alive can make it difficult to fall asleep, especially the sounds of the acrobatic performance of rats jumping from stick to stick on the 'trusses' of the roof. Only a few minutes after we settled, I heard a loud scream in the room next to me. Then, I saw the bodyguard I brought with me running through the hallway because a rat had fallen on him.

Immediately, I heard the Lord, "You brought him to protect you. Why not talk to Me? I am with you."

It's amazing the security we find in the tangible while struggling to trust the spiritual. Because of this experience, I have often asked God to open my eyes as He did Elisha's servant so that I might see the spiritual forces surrounding me to strengthen my trust in Him.

Some of our trips were simply for restocking supplies and refreshing our souls. We traveled to Monrovia, visited the church we had planted and stayed with some Liberian friends who lived in the village or with our friends who lived on the beach. Both were like family, so we shared our time equally. The three days we spent in the city always seemed to go by so quickly. On Sunday afternoons after church, we packed up the vehicle and made our way back to Buchanan.

One weekend we loaded up the car, but it would not start. We always had problems with the mobile because we truly ran it into the ground. Therefore, I had become a mechanic of sorts and began to check the various things I had learned could go wrong.

Nothing. The car simply would not start. We walked to a mechanic friend down the road to come and take a look at the vehicle. Curfew was in effect, and if you did not pass a certain checkpoint by a certain time, you would have to sleep on the road. I had this happen to me before, and since Andrea was with me on this trip, I did not want it to happen this time. Time was now of the essence, and if it did not get fixed, we would have to stay the night.

The mechanic checked this and that to no avail. I would always watch in order to learn a thing or two, but it was almost like staring at Chinese script. No matter how long you stare at it, words will not come! In any case, the car would not start.

The next day, we tried again. We labored all morning testing different things by removing various pieces and putting them back, but the car would not start. I was stressed out. No one in Buchanan knew we were staying this long, and I was concerned that people would be worried about us thinking we were stuck on the road. With a hint of frustration, I slammed the door shut. We laid our hands on the car and prayed. It started! Seriously, it just started! You would think I would have gotten the lesson by now.

We left the car running and loaded it again. We were off to Buchanan. We had plenty of time to make it before curfew as we started on our journey. Upon arriving in Buchanan, we pulled onto our familiar dirt road from the main street. Within a block from our home, people from the church ran to the road to meet us and piled on our car.

# THIS MEANS WAR

Everyone was crying, and we thought for sure someone had died. One of the ladies opened the door when I pulled off to the side of the road. She pulled me out of the car, turned and put me on her back and began jumping up and down. This is traditionally the way Liberian women rejoice when they have not seen someone for a long time. I was confused. We could not understand anything anyone was saying. At this point, we thought they were simply happy we had returned. It had been only a day, but I guess I was thankful to be back as well. I went along with the moment and thanked the Lord we were safely home.

I then heard a woman say, "Praise God you are alive!"

The statement struck me as odd.

"What happened?" I said.

"The rebels came into town last night and killed eight people," she said. "The child soldiers wanted to kill you because they said you gave them expired medications, and they thought you were trying to poison them."

I was stunned. I asked her to repeat what she had just told me, and she repeated the story verbatim.

"I have to go to the rebel base," I told Andrea as we drove home. I was afraid that if they continued with this false notion that they would still try to find me, and kill me. I figured the best way to handle this was to face it head-on. Johnny and I got in the car. Other men wanted to join us, but I told them to stay behind.

We drove behind enemy lines and went straight to the main checkpoint. I got out of the car, and I could hear the rebel boys shouting, "Chelow now come!" (Translated: Chet Lowe is here!)

The code name for the commander of that base was Black Jesus. I am unsure how he got that name, but it was all I knew him by at the time.

"Go get Black Jesus," I asked the boys, and he approached me with pomp and circumstance. I stood my ground.

My heart was racing, but outwardly, I tried to appear calm. The rebel boys were like a pack of dogs. If you showed them fear, they attacked, but, if you did not let them see you sweat, they would leave you alone. Black Jesus walked toward me, and I thought my heart would pound out of my chest.

"You know we are looking for you?" he asked with an arrogant tone.

I prayed and then said, "Looking for me? I am looking for you. I heard you wanted to kill me. I heard you think I gave you bad medication. Prove it to me," I insisted, holding my ground.

Our banter went back and forth, and as I explained the truth of the situation, the tension began to ease. Someone had used my name as a ticket to cross the rebel checkpoint. Because we had made so many trips, other groups used the fact that they knew me to endorse their ministry. This was fine with me; but, unfortunately, one of those groups distributed expired medication. The rebels blamed me for secretly trying to poison them. Everyone had become conspirators in the war. Once they understood the facts, the boys were instantaneously my friends again.

Black Jesus advanced into the room and said, "I'm sorry."

I used the moment to teach them.

"If you had killed me, you would not have been able to say sorry to me," I said as I sat with them on the porch. It felt like I was doing Sunday school, but I could not believe the topic of concern was my very life. How classic is that?

On our way home, Johnny and I marveled at the events of the day. When we got back to the house, I got out of the mobile and slammed the door. The sound of the door reminded me of slamming it the day before when the car would not start. With the gentle breeze blowing in my face, I could hear those familiar words again, "I am with you."

Slowly, I started to realize that each of these journeys was proving to me one simple point: Jesus would never leave or forsake me. In one sense, I began to feel invincible. Not that I didn't think anything could happen, I just realized that it could not happen without His permission.

*From one journey to the next, in each step of faith, He is with me,* I thought.

# SAFE IN THE STORM

*"The Lord also will be a refuge for the oppressed, a refuge in times of trouble.
And those who know Your name will put their trust in You;
for You, Lord, have not forsaken those who seek You."—Psalm 9:9-10*

## 1996

We had decided that Andrea, AJ and Micaiah would go to Monrovia while I went on my trip to Ghana. Grandpa Syl and I caught a flight out of Spriggs Payne airstrip to Accra. This was the first time I had taken a trip out of the country leaving Andrea behind. Liberia had seemed to settle, yet we felt it safer to bring the family to the capital while I was gone.

There was so much need in Liberia. Among so many lame and crippled, Jesus chose to go to one man at the Pool of Bethesda and heal him. I have often wondered why the Word does not report that He healed anyone else. I have come to believe that Jesus was completely directed by His Father. His course was planned, and there was only one man He was meant to heal at the pool that day.

It is so easy to get distracted from your calling. With so many needs and so many opportunities for ministry, it can be a challenge to stay focused on your mission. Paul began many of his letters with, "Paul, an apostle..." or "Paul, a bondservant of Jesus Christ...." He knew who he was and what he was supposed to do.

I knew I had been called to plant churches and minister to child soldiers, but many were hungry, needed shelter, and a means of survival. I got involved with all kinds of relief projects from building bridges to empowering farmers with seed and tools.

# LIVING PARABLE

We fished, farmed, traded red oil and did whatever else was needed to help those around us. These attempts to save the world led me to Ghana. As a ministry, we had decided to get involved with commercial fishing. Fish is the sustaining meat of the Liberian coastland people. Thus, our heart was to spark the local market by providing fish in exchange for red oil and reintroduce the normal trade that was devastated due to the war. The UN had given us a $15,000 grant to purchase a Fanti Canoe, nets, an outboard motor, and various supplies.

The Fanti people are a coastland people that originated from Ghana. You can find pockets of their influence up and down the West African coast as they are more directed by the currents of the ocean than the borders of man. They are skilled, generational fishermen that retain their heritage in whatever country they choose to live. The Fanti canoe is aptly named as it was designed by these tribal people. It is a carved-out log that is twenty-five to forty feet long. Once the hull is made, the sides are reinforced with structural beams that build up the depth of the canoe to allow for the daily catch to be retained. The canoes are fancifully painted with all kinds of colors and usually have some kind of scriptural quotation on the side that is believed to ensure safe travel.

The nets are placed in a center compartment and pulled out when needed. An outboard engine is attached to a small platform that jets out from the canoe on the rear of the vessel. The captain usually mans the helm and decides where to fish, while the mates on board learn from this older seadog the tricks of the trade. It's a fascinating subculture.

With money in hand, Grandpa Syl and I decided that the best place to purchase one of these boats would be in Ghana. We planned to leave for one week, purchase the vessel, and have it delivered by sea the following week with Grandpa Syl on board to ensure arrival. It was as simple as 1, 2, 3. Within a couple of days, the Lord directed our paths to secure the skiff and be ready to return on time. I would leave Grandpa Syl in Accra to make the final arrangements and return to Liberia via Abidjan, the capital city of the Ivory Coast. While there, I planned to meet two other missionary friends that were coming to serve with us in Liberia for one year.

Drew, a seventy-year-old World War II veteran, was coming to help me build and establish a HAM radio. This would allow us to have better communication with those back home. The Internet was unheard of at that time. Sheri, a young lady from our home church in Fort Lauderdale, was coming to support Andrea and teach at the elementary school in Buchanan. We had planned their arrival with my trip so that I could help bring them to Liberia for their first time.

They arrived on Good Friday, and we planned to leave the following day. When we returned to the airport on Saturday to depart for Liberia, the airport attendants laughed at us when we asked if the flight to Monrovia was on time. One of them said in broken English, "Have you not listened to BBC?" As best he could, he then described to us that war had broken out in Liberia; and the airport had been burned.

I thought for sure that this was not the case, and we went back to the hotel. I had expected to return to the airport the following day since flights got canceled on a regular basis in Africa. I assured my new missionary friends that there was nothing to worry about and that we would have one more night of bliss before entering our mission field.

I turned on the news in my room at the hotel. Sure enough, CNN was reporting that war had erupted in the capital city; and all I could think of was Andrea and the kids. Immediately, I called Andrea's parents to ask if they had heard from her. They sounded extremely concerned and explained that she had called saying that a full-fledged attack was underway. Her parents strongly encouraged me to do something quickly.

*What was I going to do?* I fell on the floor and asked the Lord to direct my steps. I prayed that the airport would open the next day and that all of us would be able to fly into Monrovia first thing in the morning. This was not the case. When we returned to the airport the next morning, no one was there, and all flights to Monrovia had been canceled. I began to feel somewhat despondent.

# LIVING PARABLE

My new friends were looking at me for our next moves, and I did not have the slightest idea of what step to take. God seemed silent, and things were not turning out the way they should.

It was Easter morning and the only thing I could think to do was to call my pastor. Our church had just finished a stadium service, and as he tells it, he was flipping hamburgers in the backyard enjoying his Easter Sunday. When he picked up the phone, I went straight to the problem. I told him all that I knew since he was not aware of the crisis in Liberia either.

At the end of my monologue, I cried, "What do I do?"

"If there is a fire between my wife and me, I am going to get burned," he said.

That was all I needed, and I began to make a plan to get to Liberia. The following day, I made arrangements with a local missionary friend to house Sheri. Drew had decided the night before that he was going with me to rescue Andrea. Neither of us knew what that meant, but we knew we had to get closer to the Liberian border. Therefore, we went to the local bus station to purchase tickets for a town located as close to the border as we could.

I was not an American at the time and only had a Bahamian passport. All transportation services required foreigners to show their passport, but my visa had expired as I was supposed to leave the previous Friday. Drew purchased the tickets with his American passport, and we were good to go.

The bus station reminded me of an anthill after you step on it; people were swarming everywhere trying to get from place to place. We must have looked confused, and Jesus sent an angel to guide us to our bus. We thanked the young lady, gave the driver our tickets and found a seat. Within a few moments of sitting down, I felt a tear at my hand resting on the window. Someone had run by, snagged my watch and took off. I have not worn a watch since. This trip was not starting well, and I did not feel good about it. I had no idea how my family was doing. I was an illegal alien in an African country.

# SAFE IN THE STORM

I was sitting beside a man I hardly knew on a bus headed to a town I had never been to before, and my watch had just been stolen. Somewhere along the line I began to wonder if I was Job! Several hours into our journey, the bus was stopped at a checkpoint. I found it unusual to have a checkpoint in Ivory Coast since they were not at war. These were immigration officers, and they were looking for people like me.

Passengers were pulled off, and their documents inspected. One young man was beaten on the head with a stick by one of the officers and apparently told to lie on the ground. Everything was in French, so it was completely foreign to me. One of the immigration officers came on the bus. He walked down the aisle and asked people to disclose their documents. One by one, he checked each person's papers and made his way back to me.

My visa had expired.

I started to sweat.

I was unsure what to do.

I could not speak French to explain my situation; besides, he did not appear to be in the mood to hear what I had to say. All I could do was pray.

When he arrived at our row, Drew pulled out his passport revealing the American seal on the cover. The immigration officer did not have him open it. I looked up, and he looked at me. I started digging around in my bag to find my passport, grabbed it and started to hand it to him. The moment was surreal. Everything you can imagine was swirling in my brain. He tapped me on my head with his stick as if to patronize me and walked away.

I could not believe it. There were neither questions nor an interrogation. I was not being hauled off the bus and put into jail. He simply walked away. The Holy Spirit is so right when He tells us to take every thought captive. All I could think was that my passport was the same color as Drew's, but the Bahamian seal on mine had worn off. As far as he was concerned, I was another American. And as far as I was concerned, I agreed!

# LIVING PARABLE

We continued our journey and arrived at our destination late that evening. We found lodging at a small guesthouse and slept well that night. Early the next morning, Drew and I were up and walking to the coast. In my mind there had to be a Fanti community there since it was a coastal village. Having just learned a great deal about this people group in Ghana, I figured we could charter a canoe to take us to Liberia. Going by road would be deadly, and besides, the borders were closed. I was amazed at how God had educated me on this form of travel to prepare me for what was ahead.

The Lord was directing us through each step in prayer. Sure enough, there was a Fanti community on the coast, but there was also a Liberian refugee community in the same town.

"What are you doing?" A Liberian man asked us as we were walking, and I explained our situation.

"I'm working with the Fanti as a fisherman," he said, and Drew and I looked at each other and praised God for leading this man to us. His name was Martin, and we instantly became best friends. Martin took us to his captain to discuss our problem.

"I am not going to Liberia," said the captain as he looked at us, laughing and shaking his head. I could tell that this was a bargaining tool on his part and began the negotiations for our travel. After haggling for about an hour, we had secured our deal with a handshake, and we were set to leave the following morning. I gave the captain a deposit to purchase fuel and supplies. Drew and I went to the market to purchase our personal food items for the trip. While there, we came in contact with a Lebanese merchant who spoke English. It was refreshing to sit in his shop. He offered us tea and a small snack. He owned a textile company and listened intently to our whole story. Then, he offered to let me use his phone.

I was blessed beyond measure and called my father in the United States. We were almost a week into this nightmare, and I was surprised to hear that no one had heard from Andrea yet. Other missionaries had gotten out of Liberia, but I knew Andrea would not leave AJ, as his adoption papers were not finalized; and only Americans were allowed to evacuate.

"The pictures on TV are horrific," my father said. "Liberia is in shambles." He purposed to stay calm on the phone, but I could tell that he was extremely worried and did not know what to tell me.

"Dad, we have a plan," and as I explained, he was silent on the phone. I knew that meant disagreement, but he chose to be supportive and we prayed.

That night, Drew and I confessed to each other every sin we had ever committed. I guess we figured that we wanted to be pure before the Lord as we boarded that vessel the next day. He told me stories about World War II, and I told him stories about my life. We laughed. We cried. We became family that night.

The next morning, we went to the captain's home to prepare to leave but he was not there. We waited until noon; still, he did not arrive. We sat there until five o'clock and he finally surfaced.

"Hello," he said as he passed us by, went into his room and grabbed a bag. Exiting the front door, he looked at us as if we were wasting his time and said, "C'mon. Let's go. It's getting late."

Who was I to complain? So we followed him to the boat.

The ocean was completely flat as we set sail. Drew, myself, the captain, four sailors and a woman with her child were on board.

"It's going to take five days and four nights to get to Buchanan," he said, and I nodded. I was ready for the trip and wanted to get to my wife and children.

There was not a cloud in the sky, and the sea reflected the light of the moon like a glimmering mirror. The coastline appeared to be a waving shadow as we sailed far out into the sea. There was lightning over the land as if a storm was brewing, so I asked the Lord to hold off the storm so that we could rest peacefully through the night. Having grown up on the islands, I loved to sleep on the sea as the billows of the swell rocked me sound to sleep.

# LIVING PARABLE

The next morning the gales had picked up, and the ocean began to churn. Our forward movement was becoming difficult, and I noticed we were getting closer and closer to shore. I was unsure of traveling so closely to the beach, as we were in range to be fired upon if there were rebels in the area. The coastline was virgin beach as far as the eye could see. I am sure that I was staring at billions of dollars in a developed country but for the most part, this property was uninhabited.

It was getting late in the afternoon, and it appeared that the captain was looking for something on shore. I had noticed what seemed to be a port about four or five miles ahead. It did not take long to realize that this was our destination for the day. I had expected that we would not stop the entire five days, but the wind was blowing in our face, and it made sense to dock until the ocean was calmer.

We saw a blown up ship in the harbor as we entered the port. I was impressed with the development of this seaport since it seemed we were in the middle of nowhere. We had landed in Greenville, the capital of Sinoe County in southeastern Liberia. Drew was glad to get out of the canoe. He was tired from travel and was more of a landlubber than a seafarer.

"Smile at everyone and be friendly," I said, as I knew Drew had a way about him that only his mother could love if he did not get along with you. However, he was the most loving and loyal person when he was on your side.

A few minutes after we had gotten out of the boat, a vehicle pulled up on the waterside. Three men approached us, and I knew immediately that they were rebel soldiers. I looked over and Drew was smiling. Good, Drew!

I had not seen these men before and thought that we could be in trouble. The man who appeared to be in charge walked up to me and began asking questions after he had spoken to a few people on the beach.

"Are you Chelow?"

Drew was smiling. I did not answer.

He asked again, "Are you Chelow who takes the bullet out of the people we put them in?"

I looked at Drew and he was still smiling.

Pointing at Drew, I said, "He is!" Then quickly added, "No, I am."

The man was confused and stomped off.

Drew was still smiling.

Unfortunately, his accusation was right. There were several warring factions in the area in which we ministered in Liberia. The group before me was their enemy. When he left, a woman walked up to us and said, "Go and hide somewhere because they're planning to hurt you."

Drew was still smiling. We found an abandoned building and settled on the floor, talking about the previous night. Neither of us had gotten much rest, and before you knew it we were both asleep. Around 10:30 p.m. both of us woke up in a fright. I looked at Drew and he looked at me and said, "I know."

We both had dreamt that we needed to leave.

We went down to the seashore and saw the captain and the other travelers resting by the canoe.

"It's time to go," I said.

"No, it's all right," the captain said. "We will leave first thing in the morning." That was not the answer I wanted. So I got into the canoe to prepare the vessel to leave.

"I've grown up on the islands and I know how to operate this machine," I said, making it clear that this was our charter and it was time for us to leave. Begrudgingly, the weary crew got up from their slumber and made the rest of the preparations to go. In about thirty minutes, we had cast off and were on our way down the river headed to the ocean.

The moon was shining again but not as bright as the sun.

We came to the sunken ship in the harbor and noticed another canoe hiding behind its sunken hull. It was about the size of our canoe but filled with about thirty passengers. They silently motioned for us to move on without stopping, so we motored along to the ocean.

# LIVING PARABLE

Upon getting into the deep sea, I noticed a storm brewing on the land. The sea was as calm as the first night we had left and I figured I would pray that the storm would go away just like it did the night before. I prayed but the storm got closer.

I prayed again but the wind began to pick up. I prayed some more but the waves started to get bigger. I prayed out loud but the storm was upon us. Within minutes, the calm crystal sea had turned into a tumultuous storm. We were being tossed to and fro in the canoe. We were bailing water and the captain was trying to steer us into the waves. The sailors were cursing me and glaring in my direction as they had not wanted to leave that night in the first place. We were all throwing up. I looked over at Drew and he was hurling over the side of the boat. I begged God to stop the storm but it seemed the more I prayed, the more the storm raged. The wind got stronger, the waves got bigger and the rain beat harder.

I went to the bow of the canoe and yelled: "God, if I die out here tonight, it is going to make You look real bad. I am going to rescue my wife. Please, help us!"

The storm raged.

For almost four hours, that storm beat us terribly. Then, as quickly as it came, it was gone. We had all made it through the night, but no one talked to me for the rest of the three-day trip. In some sense, that was fine for me because I really had nothing to say.

I remember the sun rising in the morning on that new day. I had never been more grateful for a sunrise in my whole life. God is faithful, even though I was not. I felt bad for getting upset with the Lord but I was still upset that He had not delivered us.

Finally, we arrived in Buchanan. As we approached the city, I could not wait to get off of the boat. The sun had blistered every exposed part of my skin. My nose was cracked and bleeding, and my ankles were swollen and purple. We had not eaten much over the last couple of days because we had run out of food. Everyone was tired and irritable, and I could tell that the sound of the child crying was like needles to everyone's brains.

# SAFE IN THE STORM

When we got close enough to shore, I jumped off into the sea to walk to the beach. As my body hit the salt water, it felt like acid was being poured on my skin. I had forgotten about the cuts and scrapes all over me. I am sure the salt was good for my open wounds, but the disinfecting process felt like it was going to kill me.

We quickly settled accounts with the captain and I walked briskly to my house in Buchanan. My hope was that Andrea had left the city and had come back home to wait for me. Word had already gotten to our Liberian family in Buchanan that I had arrived.

Most of them met me on the road shouting my name, "Chet!"

"Where's Andrea?" I asked, but there was no news. My heart sank. I had to figure out a way to get to Monrovia. The Liberians quickly adopted Drew as part of the family and took care of him. Meanwhile, I prepared myself to go to the peacekeeping soldiers' barracks to see if there was anything they could do. As the Lord would have it, there was a battleship sailing to Monrovia the following day, and they gave me permission, along with Drew, to come aboard for the journey.

Very early the next morning we walked to the port. We waited beside the boat for several hours until the sailors were ready to sail. While we waited, I noticed a woman walking toward me. I recognized her from somewhere, but I could not recall from where. She was smiling from ear-to-ear and acted as if she knew exactly who I was.

"Brother Chet," she said.

"Yes, that's me."

"Don't you remember me?"

I was embarrassed.

I knew her from somewhere, but my mind was simply blank.

She explained, "I was the woman..." and before she could finish, it clicked, and I finished her sentence, "...who told us to go and hide."

"Yes," she said.

"How did you escape?" I said.

"I got out of the canoe that was hiding behind the boat that night."

I told her the horrific tale of how we suffered on the water with that storm. And she looked at me and said, "You are so blessed."

I did not think she heard me, so I repeated the story adding some details to make sure she knew there was nothing blessed about it.

She said again, "Brother Chet, you are so blessed."

At this point, I thought she was out of her mind. *Look, lady,* I thought to myself, *there is nothing blessed about my experience.* Surely she was suffering from PTSD and needed psychiatric attention. The trauma of the war had gotten to this poor soul, and she did not know a blessing from a curse.

"Brother Chet, none of us knew why you left that night. But when you did, the rebels came after you on the water to kill you. They carried machine guns and wanted you dead. When the storm arose, they came in afraid for their lives. The very storm you are complaining about is what God used to save your life. Brother Chet, you are so blessed."

If you had spit at that moment, I could have swum in it. I felt as if I could seep into a crack. To think I went through all of that to learn of the loving nature of our Father. So many times we think that the Lord is out to get us. We place on Him our nature, instead of learning His and trusting Him with all of our heart.

He is our Deliverer and is always working on our behalf to reveal His loving heart towards us. At times, it may seem contrary to what we feel is true because of the circumstance. However, God is love, and that will never change.

Jeremiah says that He is a dreaded warrior always fighting on our behalf (Jeremiah 20:11). Isaiah reminds us to "Fear not" because God is with us (Isaiah 41:10). Paul explains that nothing can separate us from the love of God (Romans 8:35). We must purpose to set our minds on these precepts of Scripture so that we do not believe the lie of the enemy.

The truth remains, "We know all things work together for good to those who love God, to those who are the called according to His purpose" (Romans 8:28).

# COMPASSION FATIGUE
# IS A DISEASE

*"But I want you to know, brethren, that the things which happened to me have actually turned out for the furtherance of the gospel, so that it has become evident to the whole palace guard, and to all the rest, that my chains are in Christ; and most of the brethren in the Lord, having become confident by my chains, are much more bold to speak the word without fear."—Philippians 1:12-14*

## 1996

Monrovia was burning! As Andrea stood on a hill and looked over at the city, she could see smoke rising and hear the sound of gunfire. The city was under full attack. The place she was staying was only about seven miles from the heart of the crisis. Rebel boys were driving cars and pickups on the road in front of her as if they were on patrol. She was living in the midst of anarchy and fear haunted her at every turn.

I remember the moment we said goodbye at the airport. I could tell that she was concerned but was standing strong in support of her husband. Years later, we discussed those moments, and she told me that as she watched me take off in the airplane, she felt very alone. Holding Micaiah and AJ, she still felt the tear of a wife from her husband in simply not being together.

For over a week, no one heard from Andrea. On the last phone call with her parents, she had to hang up quickly because she did not want them to hear the rebel gunfire outside. Moreover, simple calls were too difficult to make because the only phone in our area was across the street from where she was staying. This may sound easy enough, but crossing the street meant risking your life. In war, there are no guarantees or thought for human life. Rebels were like sharks in a frenzy, and the pull of a trigger was as easy as blinking.

# LIVING PARABLE

Every night, Andrea and my boys would huddle in one room of the house of the Liberian family with whom they stayed. She was determined not to leave because without AJ's adoption papers, she knew no one would believe he was our son. Micaiah was only a year old and the Liberians had nicknamed him, "MiCRYah." He cried almost twenty hours out of the twenty-four-hour day. Between the tension of the environment and his constant tears, Andrea was solely leaning on the Lord to make it through.

She was afraid.

She had never experienced such horrific chaos. Her early years were spent in the Midwest, but from the age of eight, she had grown up in South Florida. She had learned not to be afraid for 'God is with us,' but, in this case, faith and feeling did not seem to match. She cried out daily to the Lord in prayer, and one morning she read Psalm 56. David wrote, "When I am afraid, I put my trust in you."

This Scripture inspired Andrea. She realized she was in the company of the great warrior, King David, in regards to fear. In some sense, she no longer felt alone. She came to understand that fear motivated her to put her faith into action and call upon God to rescue and save. In that sense, fear is an indicator light on the dashboard of life to remind us our trust 'valve' is not working. Knowing the problem became part of her solution.

"Andrea, you have to leave," our missionary friends told her, so she felt torn. Every fiber of her being wanted to get out of there, but she did not want to leave the family with whom she was staying. So she asked the Lord to direct her path and prayed, "Lord, if You want me to leave, have the family I am staying with tell me to go."

That afternoon it happened.

"Andrea, you have to leave," the family told her. "You are putting our lives in danger." Because Andrea and Micaiah are white, the rebels could think that she had money and torture the family until they produced it. They were also concerned about feeding three more people because the food supply was running low.

# COMPASSION FATIGUE IS A DISEASE

Andrea took this from the Lord and left that day with other missionaries who were picked up by a troop of US Marines. Traveling around the city, they were taken to a military base where evacuation operations were being conducted. Helicopters would arrive, names would be checked, and passengers would board the airlift and be taken to safety. There was only one problem—AJ did not have papers.

As her name was called, Andrea cried out in fear to the Lord, "Lord, help me!"

As she approached the US Marine that was checking all of the passengers, he asked her, "Who is this?" and pointed to AJ.

She told him, "This is my son."

"Where are his papers?" He asked.

"Burning in Monrovia," she said.

He glanced behind him and said to her, "Get on board. They will deal with you on the other side."

Andrea obeyed and ran to the helicopter without a moment's hesitation. At that exact time, my mom was on her knees praying. She always knew in her heart that our travel to Liberia would entail this kind of crisis, which was why she was so resistant to our going. We have always called her the "prophetess" for that reason.

Back home, my mom felt the prompting from the Lord to turn on the TV. Thinking it was strange, she obeyed and watched as the picture came into focus (not like our HDTVs today). CNN was on and so was Andrea.

As the Lord would have it, CNN filmed Andrea and the boys running to the helicopter that day. Everyone knew then that Andrea was alive and well; but, unfortunately, their trial was not over. All they knew of me was that I was at sea.

My mom called the US Embassy knowing that the consular was one of our friends. Oftentimes, this precious Christian couple would host us at their home to enjoy a bit of America inside the Embassy. When we stayed with them, we called our family from their phone, so my mom had her personal number.

# LIVING PARABLE

"Chet is headed to Monrovia," she explained to them.

"There is no way for him to get there," the consular told her.

"He thinks his wife is there. Trust me, he will find a way," my mom said.

The day after, I arrived at the port of Monrovia. We had traveled from Buchanan on a battleship. The sailors had us stay in the galley and fed us along the way. This ship was much different than the vessel we had traveled in from the Ivory Coast. I felt safe and secure with such weaponry surrounding us. We told the soldiers how we had traveled from the Ivory Coast to Liberia, and they could not believe we had come in a canoe. As I listened to myself tell the story, I could not believe it either. I was amazed at the hand of God over our lives and decided the canoe was actually safer than the battleship.

Once we were off the ship, there was a UN vehicle waiting to pick us up and carry us to a "safeplace."

"Can you take me to Paynesville?" I asked the driver. Paynesville was the town where I had left Andrea. He turned to look at me and laughed.

He said, "I'm not going out there. The peacekeepers are not going out there. If your wife is there, pray for her."

"Please let me down," I said, and he laughed again.

I repeated, "Please let me out of the car!"

The European fellow slammed on the brakes.

"Goodbye," I said to Drew and got out of the vehicle.

The UN driver asked, "Are you sure you want to do this? There's a war out there."

"I'm only sure that my wife is there, and I need to get to her."

I got out of the jeep. Closing the door, I noticed that the sky was dark and rain clouds were forming. I started walking and immediately I was hit with the reality of the driver's statement, "There's a war out there."

A young boy was stabbing another boy about fifty yards in front of me, and people were firing at each other from across the street. I turned to get back in the vehicle, but it was already half a mile down the road. I ran after the vehicle.

# COMPASSION FATIGUE IS A DISEASE

"Wait, don't go!" I yelled after them, but they were too far away from me to hear my call for help. I continued running down the road because it was in the direction of a military base I knew about. When I looked, there was a "porcupine pickup" coming down the road. It was filled with child soldiers who were bent on destruction.

"There's a white man," one of them screamed, and I wished I was a chameleon and could change my color! As they got closer, I saw the driver and he was one of my former students. My fear turned to sorrow. Fortunately for me, he persuaded them to let me go, and I continued running toward the base. Thankfully, the base had not been overrun. Peacekeepers were still there.

"Please, take me to Paynesville," I begged the commander of the base.

"No," he said.

"Please, I need your help. Please take me to Paynesville," I continued to beg and even followed him down the hall as he was on his way to another meeting.

"No," he said.

I was done.

I had been on a canoe for five days and had lost about fifteen pounds by this point. I had just gotten off a battleship and had run for my life to get there. I was not in the mood for small talk.

"Look, your soldiers take their women in these vehicles all over Liberia gallivanting from town to town. You have obviously failed your mission as we are at war, and I am asking you to correct this mistake by taking me to get my wife."

I was instantly escorted out of the building.

I was alone. I had no place to go. With the way everyone was talking about the area where I had left Andrea, I thought for sure she was dead. I did not know that only the day before she had flown out of the very base where I was standing. The only hope I had in mind was to brave the war and walk to Andrea, so I left the base and started retracing my steps.

About 500 yards from the base, I heard the sound of a convoy coming down the road. When I turned to see who it was, I saw an American flag. I could have started singing the national anthem. There was a heavy tank leading the convoy with three armored vehicles in tow. They screeched to a halt in front of me and opened the door, and I jumped inside one of the armored cars.

They asked, "What are you doing?"

I began to explain my plight, and we were interrupted by a call on the radio telling us that the road was clear. We quickly sped off.

They were headed back to the US Embassy. What I saw that day rocked my world! We had to travel through the center of town where the aftermath of war was gruesomely evident. Bodies were lying all over the street. They were bloated from the sun and hardly recognizable as human beings. Buildings were burning everywhere. Gunfire sounded, and a few people were pillaging stores that had been destroyed due to the fighting.

When we reached the Embassy walls, they started asking for everyone's passport. I was only holding a Bahamian passport at the time and wondered what this would mean for me. Suddenly, a rebel car came up the hill, and it was apparent they were looking for trouble. The doors of the Embassy flung open and our truck entered. From that point, I was an American whether I was or not.

When I got down from the vehicle, a woman I knew saw me and came to greet me. I was exhausted. I was not in the mood for small talk nor did I have the patience for frivolity. My world was coming to an end in my opinion, and only news of my wife and children would revive me.

The woman began to cry.

"The rebels broke into my apartment and stole my purse," she said.

I was blank.

"My passport and jewelry were inside my purse along with my wallet, and I've lost everything," she said to explain her trauma.

With every bit of concern I could muster, I lovingly said to her, "Does it look like I care?"

Indignantly, she looked at me and said, "You are obviously suffering from compassion fatigue."

There you have it—I have a disease!

# COMPASSION FATIGUE IS A DISEASE

The woman walked away, and I moved toward the embassy building where people were being processed for evacuation. The consular was there and greeted me. She could not believe I had arrived. There was not much time for conversation, so we both got straight to the point.

"Andrea was evacuated yesterday and your parents have just called. I told them to call back, but you can go ahead and use the phone to call them," she said.

I called my father and said, "This is Chet."

He did not hear me clearly and said, "What happened to him? Is he dead?"

I said, "No, this is Chet. I'm alive. I made it."

I believe my mom had passed out as I heard him say, "Wake her up, he's alive!"

We talked for a few minutes. "Andrea is well," he said. He knew her phone number.

I immediately called her, and when I heard her voice after three weeks of separation, my whole body went limp. It was as if I had been tied in knots and finally released from anxiety by hearing her voice.

It took us a week to get reunited in the Ivory Coast. She was at the airport with the boys, and we embraced for a long time. The boys did not recognize me and were actually afraid. I had lost about twenty-five pounds and had a long beard. After I had washed up, we were quickly back to best buddies.

"We have to go back to Liberia," I told Andrea on our way back from the airport. My statement surprised her, and the feelings of fear began to creep into her heart like an evil shadow in the dark. She had no thoughts of returning, and the fact that I mentioned it on the way home from the airport did not help.

Within a couple of days, our board president, Bill Pallowick, flew out to meet us in Abidjan. I can honestly say that he saved our lives. We were a mess. We should have had some kind of debriefing, but we were simply on our own. In fact, one night the boys were afraid that rebels were coming to get them.

# LIVING PARABLE

"Angels are watching over you," I explained to them. We prayed together, and then I left their room so they could sleep. About five minutes later, we heard a bloodcurdling scream come from their room. Andrea and I ran inside to find AJ and Micaiah standing up on the bed with their backs to the wall. AJ was pointing to the fluorescent lights that were still aglow. With terror he screamed, "Dad, there are angels in the room!"

We were a mess. Our kids were even afraid of angels! We decided to take a walk the following day to get some ice cream, and relieve some of the tension we were feeling. As a family, we were holding it together, yet individually, we were all stressed out.

We entered the ice cream shop and it was so distinctively normal. We relaxed and enjoyed the moment of licking cones and laughing about silly jokes that we told each other. Suddenly, Micaiah started choking. He had accidentally swallowed a piece of ice cream cone, and it had lodged in his throat. He could not cough it up. He was turning blue, and his cough had turned to a high-pitched wheeze. I went straight into lifeguard mode and began procedures to dislodge the piece. In about fifteen seconds, the wedged piece of cone flew out of his mouth, and he gasped for air. We could not believe it! Here we were in an ice cream shop and our child almost died.

That night we remembered something my aunt had told me right before we left for Liberia. She was trying to encourage us and said, "The safest place to be is in the center of God's will, no matter where in the world you are."

We knew that God had protected our lives through a war. God had protected our lives in an ice cream shop. God is our Protector. Wherever we go or whatever we do, God is with us. In this, we knew we would be in the center of God's will to go back to Liberia. It wasn't that we were not afraid, we just knew the One who hears our cries.

[From top to bottom] 1. Taken in front of our outside kitchen, AJ, Andrea, Micaiah and I are ready for church. 2. The canoe we used to travel from Ivory Coast to Liberia. 3. Kids loved the game "Duck, Duck, Goose" at Sunday school. 4. Our first church building in Buchanan.

**[From left to right clockwise]**
1. Myself and one of our boys from our child soldier ministry. 2. Village visits took hours of walking but well worth it. 3. Our baptisms at the lake in Buchanan. 4. Andrea is in front of the house we stayed at with dear friends. 5. The monkey given to us by the child soldiers. 6. The US embassy wall during the height of the war in Liberia. 7. This was AJ when we first adopted him.

# RAISING REBELS

*"The Spirit of the Lord is upon Me, because He has anointed Me to preach the gospel to the poor; He has sent Me to heal the brokenhearted, to proclaim liberty to the captives and recovery of sight to the blind, to set at liberty those who are oppressed."—Luke 4:18*

## 1998

The hardest part of returning to Liberia after the April 6 War was to discover that Albert was dead. It was very difficult to believe, but the reality of war became apparent with this physical finality. There were rumors swirling that he had stolen money and fooled around with his commander's girlfriend, and that the doctor allowed him to die. I am sure that the truth was somewhere in the middle of all of these stories. However, there is one thing of which I am sure—Albert was the thief on the cross.

After he had been shot, he was brought to the hospital in Buchanan. The bullet had entered through his lower back and exited his upper chest. There was a lot of internal damage, and quite frankly, the physicians in the area did not have the proper equipment or knowledge to do much for him. Johnny heard that Albert had come to town. I was not in the country, but he knew my heart for this young man and would visit him daily in the hospital. Other rebels would be in the room with him to say farewell to their friend, and Johnny knew the time was short.

On the last day of Albert's life, Johnny was able to share the gospel with him. Death was imminent. There was no act, opportunity for baptism or good deed he could do. All Albert did that faithful morning was receive the gift of God in Christ Jesus. He died shortly after that.

# LIVING PARABLE

There is one truth I know: I will see Albert again in the land of the living. My heart ached and rejoiced as Johnny shared this story with me. As King David understood when his child died, I knew that he could not come back to me but that one day I would go and be with him. I had made a commitment to Albert that I wanted to keep.

"If anything ever happens to you, I will take care of your younger brother, Emmanuel," I'd told him. I did not understand the implications of that statement at the time; however, the reality of the situation caused it to burn in my heart as an indelible mark that would determine my next steps of faith.

I knew what I had to do. I had to raise Emmanuel as my own son. This thought was not something I wanted to do but something I felt I had to do—not just because of the statement I had made to Albert, but because I sensed this was God's direction. Little did I know that God would use Emmanuel to change my life forever.

I had made this commitment to Albert because he had saved my life. On one of my trips into the bush, I had worn dark sunglasses that, according to the rebels, resembled a military agent in one of the Rambo movies. A rumor began to spread amongst them that I was not a missionary, but on reconnaissance for the CIA. This falsehood reached the "top brass" of the area, and I was placed on "trial" to discover if this was the case. One of Albert's commanders was the judge and jury. He was convinced that I was providing information to the enemy and wanted me dead.

Albert knew me. He had seen my ways and manner. He knew there was no possible way anyone from the CIA could make as many mistakes as I had. He spoke for me and convinced the commander that I was only a missionary by emphasizing my frailties. In an expression of gratitude, I told Albert that I would care for his brother if anything ever happened to him.

Emmanuel was rough. He had been fighting since he was very young because his older brothers had recruited him. He had worked his way up the ranks and was even working for a company as the head of security at a very early age. Several businessmen had taken the risk of exploiting the resources of Liberia during the war and would hire child soldiers to protect their assets. They paid them generously and financed part of the crisis that enabled the warlords to continue. It was a travesty, but this was Emmanuel's life.

There was a rumor stirring that the rebel soldiers were going to kill Emmanuel to inhibit him from a revenge killing. I knew time was of the essence and went behind the lines to find him. Emmanuel was stubborn; he was at his "post" and did not want to leave. Driving back, I was relieved in some ways and believed I had done what I was supposed to do. We were fostering several children at the time and quite content with the current dynamic of our family.

Over the following days, the Lord did not allow me to rest. I was content in my flesh but not in my spirit. I knew what I had to do and went back into the bush.

"Emmanuel, come and be part of our family," I said.

"No," he said, refusing again.

When I returned home, Andrea and I prayed that the Lord would do a miracle if He wanted this child to be a part of our family.

The following week, I went back into the bush again to try once more to get Emmanuel. At the beginning of the trip, I stopped to get something to drink at a local food store, and Emmanuel was at the counter. I was taken aback but acted cool.

"I'm going into the bush and will be back in three days," I said. Even though I was only going to get him, I did not tell him that. "If you want to stay at my home until I return, I can send a message to my wife. Do you want me to?"

"Yes," he agreed. I wanted to jump but remained calm.

I drove away from the store and had no idea why I was going into the bush since the point of it was to ask Emmanuel to stay with us. I guess I figured I did not want him to think that my plans revolved around him, and I wanted to keep the upper hand in our relationship.

# LIVING PARABLE

The trip turned out to be an incredible time of ministry, but I was eager to get back to the house to be with Albert's younger brother. I prayed that the Lord would do something in him to make him want to stay.

I returned home three days later, and Emmanuel was at the house waiting for me. "It's been an interesting weekend," said Andrea, who added that she would explain later.

"I'm suffering from a physical ailment that needs attention," he said, and I could sense his heart was beginning to soften.

Using that as my opportunity to show him the love of Christ, I said, "Why don't you stay the night? I'll take you to the hospital in Monrovia to see if they can help you."

Emmanuel needed surgery, so he stayed the night in the hospital and had the operation the next day. When he came out of surgery, I gave him a note that my wife had written to him. In the note, Andrea wrote that she believed God had given him to us as a gift. She invited him to be a part of our family. Since then, Emmanuel has been our son and the relationship he and his mother have is bar none.

When God asked me to minister to child soldiers, I did not know it would involve raising them as my children. There is no parenting book on what to do with a rebel child who has pillaged, raped and killed people. Andrea had explained the new dynamic in our home that she discovered the weekend I asked Emmanuel to stay.

That dynamic had to do with Saturday, another boy we were fostering. His story was another tragedy of the war. He was living in the displacement camp trying to survive. While there, he contracted pneumonia and came to the "missionary house" (to us) to get some medication, and never left.

During his recovery, he told us several stories of his life. He had grown up in a small village deep in the bush. His family members were hunters and farmers. When the war broke, his father died of a sickness, and he was left to take care of his mother and sisters at an early age.

# RAISING REBELS

He would travel to the seacoast, collect salt water, boil it and make salt for his family to sell at the market. He knew how to survive. One day upon returning from the coast, he saw smoke rising from his village. He ran to discover what had happened. He found his best friend beheaded, others killed and the village completely ransacked.

He knew that rebels had attacked and taken off down the hill to get away. Having run only a few hundred yards, he was ambushed by them. They had captured his sister as well and put a gun in her mouth to force him to join their faction. Without a second thought, he became a child soldier, and the rebels took him back to their base to train him.

On their journey home, another faction ambushed the rebels. One of their soldiers was shot, and the boys required Saturday to carry him home. The young boy died on Saturday's back that day, and he was forced to take him all the way to their base in order to bury him.

Saturday was given a gun. For the next two weeks, they trained him to fight. He was taken on a raid as part of his training and was terrified in the battle. One night, while on guard at the base, he fell asleep with his gun in his hand. When the commanders discovered him sound asleep, they beat him mercilessly to the point that Saturday thought he would die. Terrified and afraid, Saturday made a plan to run away and escape from the hands of his oppressors. Successful, he came to Buchanan, and that is where we found him.

The new dynamic in our home was that Emmanuel was Saturday's oppressor. By God's design, He had placed Simon, the Zealot, and Matthew, the tax collector, together in our home. These two disciples were enemies as one was supportive of Rome and the other was their rival. It is amazing to me that Jesus would say to each of them, "Come and follow Me," when He knew their disdain for each other. This dynamic now existed in our home.

Many people have explained to me their family problems. Often, I show a picture of my family in order to display the power of the blood of Jesus for redemption. We have had many trials but have learned over the years that we need to be strong in the grace of our Lord Jesus Christ for ourselves and for others regarding family and parenting. I pray we have instilled this into our children.

These two boys were the avenue through which the Lord began to form His plan in fulfilling the vision He had given us. Simple visits would not change the lives of these children in the bush. No program would work to reinstall proper values or change the heart. These boys needed a family. They needed people to tangibly show them the love of Christ in order to find healing. I knew our next step of faith would be accomplishing that task; I just needed Jesus to provide the people to come alongside us because the undertaking was too great for one family. There were thousands of child soldiers, but it would begin by helping one. I needed an army of families to come alongside us to rescue these children.

I know this may seem elementary to you, but one day as I was teaching, it hit me. The church was the answer. Those that had experienced the love of Christ would surely desire to display the love of Christ to those in need.

"Our church is going to foster child soldiers and help them come to Christ," I blurted it out in the middle of a sermon. It did not go over so well. The people had suffered gravely from these boys. They had lost family members, homes and property because of their evil deeds. The thought of helping them in the midst of the war was not their priority.

Nevertheless, I believed in my heart that the church was the answer for both these boys. The Lord had brought so much healing to my heart in ministering to the boys that lived in our home; I knew that He could do the same for the church. I figured they needed to be discipled and trained.

We held meetings and prayer services to discuss the issue, but people were afraid. They had run from these boys in terror, and now I was asking them to raise them as their children in their homes. It seemed impossible, but we pressed on.

# RAISING REBELS

Then, one Sunday, the Lord worked out His plan for His people. As worship began, a young man walked into the back of the church. I knew him. His code name was "Killer" and he was a notorious rebel. My son, Emmanuel, had fought with him during the war. When I went behind the lines, I was afraid of him. He had a way about him that produced fear in the hearts of people. The church was dead silent. They knew who he was as well because he had affected each one in some way. I taught the service that Sunday and gave an altar call. Killer was the first one out of his seat and walked toward me. I did not know what to do. I was not sure if he was on a reconnaissance mission for the rebels or if he had lost his mind. I looked at him. He stared back with dark eyes. He looked mad, frustrated and ready to kill. I was unsure of his intentions but welcomed him to come.

He came to the podium and stopped. He stood there as the song finished and looked at me to lead him in prayer. Usually, I closed my eyes for prayer, but that day, I realized the best prayers are with both eyes open!

Killer prayed to receive Christ.

When I said, "Amen," the church erupted with applause. I looked into Killer's eyes, and there was a physical transformation. Before, they were dark and cold; now they seemed to be filled with light, and he was smiling.

He started to cry. I started to cry. The church started to cry. We started to laugh. He started to laugh, and great rejoicing took place that day. Killer received new life, and we even gave him a new name, "Isaac," because he had brought us much laughter.

The Lord did something in everyone's heart through this young man. As they watched Isaac grow in the Lord, their hearts began to soften. God was raising up a small army at this church. They wanted to get involved and were ready to rescue more children. One after another, the Lord brought us child soldiers to place in people's homes. Other churches heard about what we were doing and wanted to get involved as well. Before we knew it, over 1,500 boys had been rescued and redeemed by the blood of Jesus Christ. Truly, there is power in One!

# ROLLER COASTER FAITH

*"My son, let them not depart from your eyes—keep sound wisdom and discretion; so they will be life to your soul and grace to your neck."—Proverbs 3:21-22*

## 1998-2000

It seemed as if we could never catch a break. Have you ever felt that way? I mean, you are at the place where nothing goes right, and just when you stand up, something knocks you down again. It amazes me that after Paul talks about the incredible peace of God in the first few verses of Romans chapter five, he was led to tell us: "And not only that, but we also glory in tribulations..."

This blows my mind! How do you relate the peace of God to suffering? How can you compare rejoicing in the hope of Jesus with trials and tribulations on earth? Reading further in the text, you begin to see that our "tribulations produce perseverance; and perseverance, character; and character, hope" (Romans 5:3-4).

Paul realized that because everything around us is simply a reminder that this place is not our home. Life's circumstances are used by the Lord to further shape us into the image of His Son Jesus Christ. He will never disappoint us because nothing will separate us from His love, "Neither things present nor things to come..." (Romans 8:38).

It took me a while to get this. At times, I had lost hope and the Lord seemed like a battering ram trying to break through the walls of my heart. Like Paul, we were "in journeys often, in perils of waters, in perils of robbers...in perils in the city, in perils in the wilderness, in perils in the sea, in perils among false brethren, in weariness and toil, in sleeplessness often, in hunger and thirst, in fastings often, in cold and nakedness" (2 Corinthians 11:26-27).

# LIVING PARABLE

When I read this Scripture, I thought to myself that Paul must have visited Liberia. Yet, for some reason I was comforted that this was in Scripture, and the Holy Spirit was trying to tell me that this was normal. This lesson has been reinforced in my life through each trial He has allowed to touch us. Truly, it has taught me to say, "We also glory in our tribulations." However, this lesson took some practice.

At the end of three years in Liberia, Andrea and I were tired. The constant pangs of war coupled with sickness made us long for home. We were starting to dream of ice cream. One time, I had a dream that I had jumped into a pool of chocolate and was eating my way out from drowning.

Seriously, we realized that our conversations began to boil down to "two all-beef patties, special sauce, lettuce, cheese, pickles, onions on a sesame seed bun...it's a good time for the great taste of McDonalds" (theme song for McDonald's hamburgers at the time). We were at a tipping point but did not know it at the time. A break would have been nice, but we decided to pummel through despite the way we felt.

Every night I drove our car to a peacekeeping checkpoint and walked home. Since thieves had attempted to steal it several times, we learned that parking it at the house was not wise. Therefore, the car was taken to its resting place for the evening, and we 'paid' the guards by providing a nightly meal. It was mutually beneficial.

One particular evening, one of our foster sons, Joe, and I were walking home. It was never a good idea to walk by yourself at night. After a long day, this mile-long walk home seemed eternal. In one sense, it was a good chance to discuss several topics, yet sheer exhaustion often overcame the desire to speak and silence prevailed.

"I've been bit!" I shouted. I shined the light and saw a black snake slithering away into the night. My worst nightmare had come to pass! Looking at my heel, I saw two puncture marks with blood softly streaming from them as it often does when getting an injection at the doctor's office.

"Don't panic!" Joe said.

*Don't panic?* Did Joe not understand that this was my greatest fear? I could feel the stinging of the bite at this point and wondered when I would fall over dead.

"Don't let your heart rate go up!" He said, but that was impossible. I am sure it spiked to 120 beats per minute. Quickly, he lifted me up and carried me to the house. He did not want me to walk and speed the circulation of the poison. In his mind, this would help. He ran with me and placed me on the floor when we got to the house. He made a small cut next to each puncture and began to try to draw the poison from my body.

Someone went to get Andrea from our room. When she saw what had happened, she screamed, ran out the front door and did not return for about twenty minutes. I did not know at the time, but she ran to the local medical clinic to see if one of the French nurses stationed there would come and help.

I woke all of the children. I thought for sure that I was going to die and wanted to bless them as Jacob did in his last breaths. I prayed over each one and sat back wondering what would happen next. Andrea came back breathing heavily with a French nurse in tow.

As I look back, the scene was hilarious. My children were wondering when I would go into convulsions and die while this French nurse was struggling to speak English and ask me some questions.

With a book in her hand, she asked, "Do you feel this?"

I replied, "Yes." She sighed with concern.

She asked another question, "Do you feel this?"

I replied, "Yes." She sighed with concern again.

Finally I said, "Can we just pray?"

By God's grace, I survived the night. Obviously, I survived the bite. The next morning, none of the typical symptoms were apparent. A doctor told me that quite possibly the snake and I simply crossed paths, and he bit me to get out of the way. My life was saved since there was not much poison in his fangs. One way or the other, I knew in my heart that God had spared me.

# LIVING PARABLE

*This was it!* I was ready to go home. Besides, our funds had dropped, and it seemed this was the best decision to make. We packed our bags and headed back to the United States. At this point in my life, I have learned not to make decisions when I am emotional. I would not say that I am failproof, but I have established people in my life as personal check-points before I make any major decisions. This allows time to process and get through any emotion that may be guiding my steps. Choosing to leave Liberia this way was part of the process of learning my lesson.

I was miserable at home. In Liberia, it seemed that if I spoke to a rock, water would come out. In the United States, the land seemed so dry and parched that there was no water to be found for hundreds of miles.

Ministry was different; people had changed, and the term "re-entry" was never discussed with me. Besides, we had left for Liberia with one child, Micaiah, and came home with five. At this point, we had adopted Saturday, Emmanuel and AJ, and Andrea had given birth to Abigail, our first daughter.

Within months, I wanted to return. I figured I had partaken in rest, McDonalds and ice cream to the gills, and longed for the opportunity to go into the jungle and save child soldiers. I remember a friend telling me that my greatest step of faith would be staying and not going. She was right. Remaining in the States was a struggle that I did not want to overcome.

Day after day, I sat daydreaming about being back in Liberia. I was working at our church at the time, and it seemed that nothing was going right. First, I was going to have one position, and it changed. Then, I was going to have a different role, and it changed. These transitions began to speak louder than words to my soul, and I concluded: Why would I stay where there is no need for me when there are so many in Liberia to whom I could minister?

One morning in my devotions, I read a Scripture that seemed to point toward going back to Liberia.

# ROLLER COASTER FAITH

"I'm so excited that God had spoken to me for us to return," I told Andrea. As always, she was willing to go, and we prepared our family to pack up and head back. News that we were returning to the mission field began to spread. While walking in the halls at church one day, one of the ladies who worked there asked, "Are you sure that God is not answering you according to your idols?"

I thought that was preposterous. He spoke to me in His Word. We returned with joy! From the first day we arrived, Liberia was hard. Things had changed over the year of our absence. People had changed, and we were surprised at the opposition we were facing in ministry. No longer was I speaking to the rock; I was frustrated and hitting it more often than not.

One night, I woke up to hundreds of snakes on my bedroom floor. They were slithering and hissing. I had no idea how they got into the house and had never seen so many snakes in one place except in an Indiana Jones movie. I looked to the foot of my bed, and a giant snake crept onto the covers and began sliding its way toward me. I was frozen in fear. I could feel its scaly body climbing up my leg and torso. Its head was diamond shaped, and its forked tongue was hissing out of its mouth. The snake's eyes were staring right at me as if to kill, and nothing was getting in its way. Slowly, it rose from the bed with neck poised in striking position. Its mouth opened wide as poison dripped from its fangs, and I could see the back of the serpent's throat. As it lunged toward me, I raised my hands to grab the neck of the snake, shouting at the top of my voice.

At that moment I heard, "Chet, wake up! You're having a mefloquine dream again."

It was my wife.

She was reaching over, half asleep, trying to pull my arms down out of the air. Mefloquine is a powerful prophylaxis drug that fights the malaria bug in your body. Unfortunately, I experienced one of the potential side effects and got technicolor nightmares. After that night, I decided to quit taking the medication until I felt the symptoms of malaria.

# LIVING PARABLE

Whether on or off it I was still getting malaria, so I felt this was the best decision. I could not go back to sleep. I lay awake until morning pondering the dream because it seemed to have more significance than simply mefloquine. A friend of ours came to visit that day, and I downloaded to her the details of my dream. We all laughed about it and concluded our night with prayer before she left to go home. Early the next morning, our friend was knocking at the door. She seemed somewhat frantic as if something had gone wrong. We took her back to our bedroom because she seemed very distressed.

"Chet and Andrea, your dream was from the Lord. Last night, after I left you, the Lord ministered to me the meaning of your dream."

This was somewhat strange for us and seemed a little more Old Testament in nature, but she did not hesitate to continue though we must have looked confused.

"The snakes are many trials that are about to come your way. The larger snake is one trial that will seem to consume you, but take heart; you will overcome." She paused for a moment and looked at the ground and then said, "You must take the next thirty days to fast and pray. I will join you."

She was not a crazy woman, but this was strange. We were perplexed by her warning but thought to ourselves that prayer and fasting would be good for us anyway because of the trials we were facing in Liberia. Thus, we took her advice and began thirty days of prayer and fasting on March 1.

On April 1, our son Saturday woke up, and his jaws looked like jowls. His cheeks had swollen, and his appearance was abnormal. Two days later, our son Micaiah woke up with the same thing. Two days after that, I awoke with the same appearance. We had mumps! Each of us had been vaccinated prior to coming to Liberia, but there was no mistaking it; our cheeks were touching our ears. We looked like the "elephant man," and everyone in our home treated us like we had the plague because they did not want to get it.

# ROLLER COASTER FAITH

It took several days for the swelling to go down, and we were thankful to be quarantined in our house because it was too embarrassing to go outside anyway. Meanwhile, Andrea had developed a painful cough. She did not pay much attention to it at first because colds were a common part of everyday life. She thought it was simply a strong virus that would not go away. We had planned a trip into the interior for the middle of the month, and we both thought it was a good idea to keep to the plan. My swelling was no longer apparent, and Andrea seemed well outside of this cough, so we kept the plan intact.

We were going deep into the jungle. It took us several hours to get to the end of the road by car, followed by a couple of hours of walking to get to the village. We had heard there was an isolated group of child soldiers in this area. We wanted to reach out to them to see if we could share Christ and begin a relationship with them to hopefully get them out of this armed conflict.

The initial trips were always difficult. Most of the troops in this area had heard of me by this time because of our consistent visits. However, everyone was always very suspicious upon our arrival because we were at war. Trust was relative to the child soldier based on which alliance would best serve his well-being and survival. With factions constantly changing leadership, making strategic partnerships had become a skill.

We were usually well-received after the formal greetings. On occasion, it would get tense as the boys tried to show their dominance. There was not much you could do during those moments besides pray and stand your ground. They would brandish their weapons, poke at you and try to intimidate you any way they could.

I never got used to it. I believed that making the choice to go behind the lines was an act of obedience. And so, I felt that it was God's responsibility to take care of me. This does not mean that I was not afraid; I simply believed it was God's way of keeping me completely dependent on Him in order to accomplish His purposes in my life and theirs.

# LIVING PARABLE

Thankfully, this connection had gone well. It did not last more than an hour because we had learned through our experiences that the first trip should always be short and sweet. Walking back, I wished there was an easier way to get to these boys. It always seemed like such a long trip for such a short visit. As with the other locations, I knew this was the beginning of a much longer process; however, these journeys were beginning to wear on me.

About thirty minutes into the way home, I started feeling pain in my joints. I knew exactly what this meant—I had malaria. Before long, the fever had spiked to 102-103. I did not recall getting a fever earlier and thought that if I had spiked to this level in the first round, the second bout would be much worse. Everything in my body was aching. I had to sit down several times on the way to the car because every step heightened the migraine I was feeling in the back of my head. The journey back to the vehicle seemed ten times longer.

We finally arrived to the jeep. I crawled into the back seat and tried to find a comfortable position for the long ride on the dirt road to the paved road to home. As usual this time of year, dark clouds were forming, and we could smell the rain as the temperature dropped due to the cool breeze of the approaching storm.

The rain came down in sheets. It was a violent storm. In some sense, it seemed demonic. The rain was beating the car like a fighter punching a bag at the gym. Lightning cracked as thunder roared, terrifying the lady who was in the jeep with us. The driver was only going a snail's pace because it was difficult to see the road ahead, and my fever was relentlessly reminding me that I was internally hosting a party of protozoans swimming around in my blood.

Our driver came to a screeching halt. The rain had washed out the log bridge, and there was no way for us to pass. A lake of water was to our right and left. The only way to pass was to try and reform the bridge with the remaining logs and hope it would hold for us to pass.

# ROLLER COASTER FAITH

Everyone got down from the car and walked single file across one of the remaining logs to the other side. After arranging two logs parallel to each other about the width of the tires, our driver drove slowly across on what seemed to be toothpicks suspended above the waterway. Standing in the pouring rain, we all prayed out loud as he inched the vehicle to safety. Wet, burning with fever, and incapacitated due to an excruciating migraine, I rested sedately against a friend's shoulder praying to make it to the paved road.

Coming down a long hill, our driver stopped as people gathered on the road. The rain had calmed to a gentle mist, and they were trying to discover if we would take any passengers into town. Since our vehicle was full, they started to wave us on.

"Does anyone have any headache tablet?" He asked, as he was desperately concerned about me and wanted to relieve my pain. In that instant, a bright light shone on my face. I knew I was not dead yet and was slightly bothered that I had become the museum exhibit entitled, "White Man Dying with Malaria!"

After several observations, one of the older men standing on the road whispered to our driver, "You had better leave him here. I don't think he will make it to the road."

With every bit of energy I could muster, I reached forward, grabbed the back of the driver's seat and said, "Don't leave me here! Please, keep driving." Thanking everyone for their assistance, we pulled away, and I was relieved.

About an hour later, we made it to the paved road. There was a hospital close by that was run by dear friends of ours. I was grateful to be off the dirt road that caused the vehicle to bounce up and down, constantly jolting my pounding head. When we reached the hospital, my fever was close to 104. I was limp and was carried to a tepid bath to bring my fever down. Thankfully, it broke, and we were able to sleep there that night being heavily medicated with malaria treatment.

# LIVING PARABLE

I slept until mid-afternoon the following day. This precious family wanted me to stay and recover fully, but I was concerned about being gone another day, as I believed Andrea would worry. We loaded the car and began the three-hour trip home. I could not help but reflect on the snakes in my dream as we traveled. I was grateful that we had fasted and prayed but sensed we had not yet experienced the dreadful challenge lying ahead.

Slightly anxious, I was reminded of Philippians 4:6-7: "Be anxious for nothing, but in everything by prayer and supplication, with thanksgiving, let your requests be made known to God; and the peace of God which surpasses all understanding, will guard your hearts and minds through Christ Jesus."

This Scripture gave me great assurance. In life, there are going to be things that make us anxious. It is a natural response to some of the situations we face in our daily routine.

Jesus told us, "Do not worry." However, He has also given us the powerful privilege to pray and connect with Him to live supernaturally. This step of faith brings us to the place of peace. Quite possibly, we may begin to see things from His perspective. Maybe, we will simply feel His Presence. In any case, prayer is the practice that brings us peace. Thus, in prayer, He gave me peace!

# MINISTRY IDOL

*"No temptation has overtaken you except such as is common to man; but God is faithful, who will not allow you to be tempted beyond what you are able, but with the temptation will also make the way of escape, that you may be able to bear it. Therefore, my beloved, flee from idolatry. I speak as to wise men; judge for yourselves what I say."—1 Corinthians 10:13-15*

## 2000

I had never been so happy to pull into our driveway. Every homecoming was always exciting. The kids would come running to the car. Andrea would be smiling at the door looking as if she was ready to go out for a night on the town, and my heart would be at ease to be reunited again. Since our separation during the war, I struggled with the fear that it might happen again. Most fears are unfounded, but because this had been our reality, I would often go to the Lord in prayer to be reassured of His comfort and presence.

However, this homecoming was not welcoming at all. Only one of the boys came to the car, and he looked forlorn. I asked, "What's going on?"

"Mom does not feel well, and I think Abigail has malaria," he said.

Immediately, I jumped out of the car, still weak from the fever the day before. I got slightly lightheaded and had to pause for a moment to catch my breath. Andrea was in the room with Abigail. They were both lying on our bed and neither of them looked well. She was not aware that I had been sick, and I decided not to tell her until I could find out what was going on with her.

"My cough has gotten much worse," said Andrea. "I feel as if someone is stabbing me with a knife every time I cough. And Abigail got a fever last night and has been down for most of the day sleeping."

# LIVING PARABLE

Abigail was only five at the time. She was lying down in her blue Cinderella nightgown. She had gotten it at Disney World the previous year. As I stared at her, I recalled that trip. Abigail was a fan of Cinderella. She believed in her heart that she was a personal friend of hers because we had read so many books about the story. While we were in the park, a parade of characters came by, and Abigail had insisted that we made sure that Cinderella saw her.

Sure enough, as Cinderella passed in all of her pomp and circumstance, Abigail screamed, "Hello, Cinderella! It's me, Abigail!" Giving the traditional wave, Abigail was convinced Cinderella recognized her, and who was I to tell her otherwise?

Eliya was also lying down beside Andrea in the bed. She was only three months when we returned to Liberia and was now almost a year old. She was the first of our children to look and behave like Andrea. She did not cry much and always seemed very content. Andrea would pack this precious bundle on her back like the Liberians throughout the day. Eliya simply enjoyed the ride and would smile any time someone caught her eye.

Abigail stirred on the bed. She lifted her hands for a hug. I crouched down beside her, squeezed her tightly and whispered, "I love you." Her smile melted my heart. It was weak but sincere. I was glad to be home and stared at the two of them for most of the day as I sat in the room on our chair. Andrea shrieked as she coughed, and Abigail moaned every time she rolled over. They had both taken medications but were still recovering.

That evening, Abigail once again got a fever. We used cold compresses on her forehead and put her in a tepid bath, but nothing seemed to break the fever. She was burning up, so I held her in my arms and carried her outside to allow the cool breeze to blow on her face as we continued the compresses all over her body.

We were sitting on our porch, and Andrea started to pray. Abigail was not doing well, and we were unsure what to do. Her breathing became erratic. We decided to take her to the hospital but were concerned about the kind of care she would receive, as people did not seem to get better in these wartime clinics.

As I held her in my arms, her eyes rolled back, her body went limp, and she blew out a breath that was horrifying.

"Lord, please save our child!" Andrea cried.

I lifted my eyes to heaven and said, "Did You bring us to Africa to take my daughter? Please don't take her, O, God!"

What seemed to be hours was probably only a few seconds. Abigail inhaled a deep breath as this tiny child's body began to show signs of life. I pulled her close to me, and Andrea placed her hand on her back embracing both of us. We wept in sorrow. We wept for joy. We simply wept!

The following morning I made the decision that Andrea was going to go home with the girls, and I would follow shortly. She did not want to go as she struggled with separation the way I did. However, we did not have enough money for all of us to travel, and I had to wrap up a few things but did not feel Andrea or Abigail could wait. Andrea's cough had gotten much more intense. I remember looking at her that morning as she changed, noticing how thin she had become. Everything was taking its toll on her, and we needed to get out.

Without her knowing, I went to town and purchased plane tickets for them to leave that night. As the Lord would have it, a missionary friend was leaving on that same flight, and I met her in town as she confirmed her flights. It worked out perfectly since she agreed to help Andrea and the two girls, Abigail and Eliya. Arriving home, I sat down with Andrea and showed her the tickets. While I was gone, the Lord had ministered to Andrea that she needed to get medical attention. Jesus had prepared her heart for what I had done, and in an hour, she was packed, and I took them to the airport.

Andrea's mom flew to New York to meet Andrea and the girls. While in the air, Andrea started coughing blood. She knew that this was not just a serious cold; something else was wrong with her internally. We later learned that she had been misdiagnosed in Liberia and was suffering from pneumonia and pleurisy. This condition creates a hole in the lining that surrounds your lungs and had caused the excruciating pain.

The doctor placed Andrea on heavy medications that forced her to stop nursing Eliya. Unfortunately, no one took into account that Andrea's antibodies were protecting Eliya from sickness, and when she stopped nursing, Eliya got malaria. Three days after their arrival in Fort Lauderdale, Andrea was on medications, and Eliya was in the ICU with malaria. The boys and I were stuck in Liberia without enough money to fly home. I called Andrea every morning and evening to get an update.

On the third day she said to me, "Chet, you need to come home. I am not sure about Eliya. The doctors have her in ICU and say it does not look good." She also explained, "I went to our post office box. Three people have donated $6,000."

It was exactly what we needed for the four boys and me to fly home. We left that night. The trip home was brutal. We had only been in Liberia for six months since our return, and nothing had gone right. My wife was seriously sick, and I was not sure about the fate of my daughter who was lying in the hospital. We only had enough time to pack a small bag and left most of our things behind. My spirit was perplexed.

I walked down the aisle of the airplane to use the bathroom. Everything felt like a daze because it happened so quickly. After shutting and locking the door, I looked in the mirror and immediately heard the voice of that precious woman from several months before, "Are you sure that God is not answering you according to your idols?"

Tears began to flow down my face. I fell onto the floor of that filthy bathroom and wept. I begged the Lord for forgiveness and asked Him to spare my daughter's life. I was humbled and could only look to Him in my weakness.

When we landed in Fort Lauderdale, I was wondering what news I would face. The travel had taken almost two days because of connections, and we did not have cell phones back then. I had prepared myself to hear the worst and was shocked when we came out of the terminal and saw Andrea holding Eliya—both had been healed!

We held each other as a family for about ten minutes. I did not care that people had gathered to find out what was going on. We were home. We were together, and God had spared our lives. This proved to be our last time living in Liberia. We emphatically agreed when the doctors told us that we could not return until Andrea was completely recovered. Our board of directors decided that we could not go back for at least a year, and I chose to lay down this idol in my life of ministry. I was humbled in so many ways.

There was no fanfare. There was no reception or special parties for our homecoming. I felt like a Vietnam vet who had returned home after the crisis to a bewildered America that did not know why he had gone off to war in the first place. With all we had done and all we had been through, it was amazing the way God brought us home at the conclusion of our adventure—in humility.

In the wisdom of God, this was exactly the lesson for us. "Humble yourselves before the Lord..." is an action on our part. None of us like the character of God that "opposes the proud." It seems almost unlike God to come against us. Yet, the only reason He opposes you is to produce humility. His purpose is to fulfill the latter portion of that verse, "And He will lift you up in due season" (James 4:10 NIV).

# WEAPON OF WORSHIP

*"But at midnight Paul and Silas were praying and singing hymns to God, and the prisoners were listening to them. Suddenly there was a great earthquake, so that the foundations of the prison were shaken; and immediately all the doors were opened and everyone's chains were loosed."—Acts 16:25-26*

## 2003

Returning to Liberia for me is like going home. Friends are family. The pace slows down due to limited technological opportunities. People sit on the front porch and tell stories of their day. Relationships are valued, and constant visitors come by to share life. There is no need to call or make any plans. Everyone is welcome all of the time, any time for any reason.

Boarding the plane to return for a pastors conference in Liberia I was thinking of the greeting we would get at the airport. *"A po be nyene-o"* is a traditional Bassa greeting that means, "You are all welcome." I was taking a small group with me that would minister at the conference and visit the various churches that we had planted. I was excited for them to have this experience in Liberia since it serves to strengthen your faith in so many ways.

As expected, many friends were waiting to give the traditional welcome. Usually, there would be more people than seats in the vehicle, so the American group automatically got a good taste of Liberian culture by practically sitting on people all the way home. We were so snugly fit that if the door were to open, we would all pop out. We settled at the mission that night and prayed together as a team before going to bed. The next morning, people shouting on the road awakened us. I walked out of our house and saw people running on the street.

# LIVING PARABLE

We had been in Liberia for less than twenty-four hours and crisis had hit. As we learned throughout the morning, the UN had encouraged the rebels to turn in their weapons for fifty dollars. The plan seemed ingenious until the UN told the soldiers they would go through six weeks of training before receiving their cash, according to what we heard.

Hundreds of rebel boys with weapons had gathered in several places throughout town to turn in their weapons. Upon arrival, they told these children they would have to wait to receive their money. (Seems to me like someone did not really think that one through.) This enraged the boys and caused them to riot in angry mobs throughout the city.

A Liberian man who worked for the Christian school where we were staying, walked up the dirt path as we stood outside talking about what was happening. He was disheveled and confused. The missionaries I brought with me looked very concerned because we heard gunfire and this man was so distraught.

"What happened?" I asked.

"I was stopped at an intersection and an angry gang of young people took my car," he said. "The city is in chaos, and the rebel boys are rioting everywhere."

I knew we only had a little bit of time if we wanted to retrieve that car. There was another mission car on the property, and my thought was to go to the peacekeepers' checkpoint and inform them of the stolen car so that they could help us retrieve it. One of the missionaries named David, three Liberians and I got in the car. I figured it was safe because we were going away from the city and had just passed this checkpoint the day before when coming from the airport.

David was my assistant and the worship leader at the church we planted together. In sincerity, I could say that he is a man in whom there is no guile. He is a faithful man that loves God with all of his heart, soul, mind and strength. I was honored that he was with me. The checkpoint was about thirty miles away at a military station.

# WEAPON OF WORSHIP

About a mile from the base, we were stopped by a group of UN peacekeepers that appeared to be from a Middle Eastern country. They simply waved us on, and we continued forward. Coming up to the checkpoint, I noticed that there were no soldiers on the road. I could see hundreds of children inside the base, but the road appeared to be empty except for the UN trucks parked at the intersection of the checkpoint. I thought this was strange but continued to move forward ignoring my gut instincts.

When we stopped at the checkpoint, about a hundred boys came up from either side of the road and ambushed our car like bees on honey. We were overwhelmed in moments. Our doors were forced open, and the boys tried to rip us out of the car. I was back to back with the Liberian man sitting in the front seat with me, and we kicked and punched trying to stay inside the vehicle.

One of the boys grabbed my leg and began to pull me out of the car. I secured my arm around the steering wheel because I knew that if I were taken from the vehicle, I would not survive. I looked in the rear-view mirror and saw David being attacked as they ripped at his pockets and tried to take his clothes.

"Stay in the car!" I screamed, and he tried his hardest to oblige.

At the same time, the UN trucks we had seen parked on the side of the road were also trying to escape. I raised my hand to them to help us, yet it was obvious that they could not even help themselves. It was absolute mayhem. Everyone was fending for their own lives. It happened so quickly that there was no time to do anything but try to stay alive.

Suddenly, a young man came at me with a knife. I thought this was it. After all I had been through, I was going to die on the side of the road by a military base. He brandished his weapon and smiled at me. Somehow, I was able to shut the door. I looked in front of me to take off, and there was another kid pointing an AK-47 through the windshield at my forehead. He jumped on the hood of the car and motioned with his hand for me to quickly go forward.

Right then, our back glass was shattered. I did not know if it was a bullet or a rock, so I screamed, "David, are you dead?"

"No. GO! GO! GO!" He said, so I went. As I was moving forward, the UN was escaping in their ten-ton lorries. I barged my way in-between their convoy and made a U-turn. I knew this would mean going back through that riot, but it was the only way home, and it had to be done. The boy with the weapon was still on my windshield, and I used it to my advantage. I hid behind him so that no one could see me driving and hoped they would assume that one of them had stolen our car.

Human obstacles were now in front of me. I did not run over anyone, but I am not too sure how I managed to get through. I put my foot to the metal and went around the UN trucks that were going way too slow for my comfort. The young man on my windshield was holding on for dear life. I had almost forgotten he was there, and since I could not travel with him any further, I hit the breaks, and he slid off. I then hit the gas and we were gone. I prayed he would be okay.

The car was silent on the way home. We were all in shock. When we got back to the school, we looked like the disheveled and distraught man that had started this whole thing in the first place. I sat in the car for a moment as everyone piled out. David was waiting for me beside my door when I stood up.

"Would you like some water?" He said, looking at me nonchalant.

He was willing to lay his life down as a living sacrifice, which as Paul said, "is our reasonable act of worship" (Romans 21:1).

He was truly a worship leader. Considering this welcome to Liberia, we had to decide if we were going to host the pastors conference as most of the delegates had already arrived. Through much prayer, we sensed the Lord telling us to move forward and to keep our focus on worshiping Him, not on the situation around us.

Two of our pastors arrived the following day. They had been beaten and bloodied on the road, and I was overwhelmed that they had pressed on to come. At that point, I knew we had made the right decision; these men and women were hungry for the gospel.

# WEAPON OF WORSHIP

In our Western culture, I think we sometimes look at opposition as the Lord's hand guiding us to quit. The Liberians see it as opposition from the enemy and a challenge to press on. We started the conference with praise and worship. Liberian choruses are incredible. The drum was beating, and the people were clapping, singing songs at the top of their lungs. The missionaries enjoyed the moment. One of them was outside taking pictures of the event while the others were purposed to stay in step with the chorus leader.

I know that worship is more than just the songs we sing; it is the life we live. However, songs are a wonderful way to love the Lord your God with all of your soul. Paul wrote that we should, "Speak to each other with psalms, hymns, and spiritual songs" (Ephesians 5:19). This moment was glorious, and we were all enraptured with the music.

I was sitting up front on a side row. The church building was an old abandoned house, and they had turned the living room into the sanctuary. It could hold about 100 people Liberian style. Because I was on the side, I was able to watch everyone worship and still see out the back windows. People were so excited to begin the conference that their worship was unto the Lord.

Still staring at the back, I noticed something going on in the market in front of the church. There appeared to be some kind of commotion, but I could not tell what it was. I continued to scan the scene and realized rebels were attacking the street. It was only about fifty to seventy-five yards from our front door, and there was no mistaking what was happening.

Nancy, our worship leader, noticed it as well. She was facing the audience and could clearly see out the back window. The church continued to worship. Between the drums and the voices, they could not have possibly heard the commotion behind them.

My mind ran to an event that had happened during the war. There was a Lutheran church where over 400 people sought refuge. They believed that the rebels would not harm them once they were inside. Tragically, the rebels barricaded the people inside the church and burned them all alive. I could not get this out of my mind and though my lips were moving, my mind was not in the place of worship.

Nancy began to sing louder. She started another praise song and decided that she would be faithful to the Lord's direction. People in the church began to turn around and notice the commotion, as one person after the other tapped a shoulder for them to turn and look. I was trying to direct our missionary to come in while appearing calm as everyone was looking at me. The rebels started to approach the church. With every step closer, our worship leader sang louder. In fact, it was as though she lost sight of who was approaching and gained spiritual sight of Whom she was worshiping. I was inspired and began to sing as loud as she. I raised my voice and my hands to the Lord since He is worthy of praise! The church followed suit.

The rebels walked right up to the church and then right past us. I was sitting closest to the side they passed, and I had one eye on Jesus and one eye on them. Nancy did not look. She kept her focus on the Lord and led us to victory.

Nancy reminded me of Kenaniah, the man who led the army of Judah to victory under King Jehoshaphat. The incredible thing is that he was not a military commander but a worship leader. As history records, the king was deeply distressed over the armies that formed against him. One of the sons of Asaph, the leaders of Judah's worship, told him that this battle belonged to the Lord. In response, Jehoshaphat sent the choir to sing before the army of the Lord to lead Judah to victory. We had experienced this power in worship and were glorifying God.

When the conference was over, a group of us decided to visit one of the churches in Buchanan outside the city of Monrovia. This trip would entail passing the checkpoint at which we had been ambushed. We had heard that the coast was clear and decided to make the journey to encourage the saints who were there. However, rebel forces now controlled half of the road since the uprising. This may have seemed foolish on our end, but keep in mind, peace is relative in Africa.

# WEAPON OF WORSHIP

The night before we left, I held a meeting to discuss what I had learned about working with rebels. I explained that they were unpredictable and tried to persuade the team not to go. One of our members decided to stay, but the rest were confident this was what God was directing them to do. I was very friendly with most of the fighters on this road, as they were the ones to whom I had ministered during the heat of the war, so jokingly I said, "Be concerned if they take you behind a house!" We all nervously laughed, prayed together, and went to bed. The next morning we loaded the car and were on our way after prayer. We passed "ambush checkpoint" with no problems and were somewhat relieved. Heading toward the first rebel checkpoint, we all said a quick prayer.

As we approached, you could hear some of the boys shouting, "Che-low now come!" (Translated: Chet Lowe is here!) In a strange way, it was relieving to hear them call my name. We stopped and waited for them to direct us. Several of the boys came to the car.

"Get out of the car and follow me," one of them said to me.

As I was walking to the back of the house, I could hear Lysa, one of the missionaries on our team, bust out into tongues. In her mind, the joke from the night before had become our reality.

"What is she saying?" One of the commanders asked me.

"She has a language that only God understands," I said. "She is worshiping Him right now and asking Him to protect me. If I were you, I'd be careful." He led me back to the car, and all was well.

Worship is incredible. It gets our mind off of our limitations and ourselves and puts our heart in the right place. We worship a God who can do immeasurably more than all we ask or imagine. We were created to worship Him because He knows that as we keep our mind on Him, He will keep us in perfect peace. This peace comes because with God, all things are possible. David, Nancy, and Lysa all worshiped in different ways, but each one had the same outcome.

God was glorified!

# IT'S YOUR TURN

In case you skipped over the introduction like I usually do when I am reading a book, I want to reiterate what is probably the most important part for you to remember. These stories are written not for you to tell, but to inspire you to develop your own. In fact, even though I have taken a couple hundred pages to get the point across, the Lord sums up the direction in one simple word..."Go!"

Did you hear His voice in that one word from Matthew 28? I know you are reading a book, but I sense that many of us read the Scriptures like a book as well. Surely, the Bible is filled with good stories and miraculous events depicting incredible heroes and villains, containing wars and romance within its pages. Yet, it is undoubtedly the greatest book ever written because its authors wrote under the inspiration of the almighty God.

My concern is that after we read the adventures of the Bible, we simply shut it, place it on a shelf and walk away. We may gain the knowledge of a story, but have we understood the lifestyle to which we are called? Read it again, "GO!"

The narrative of the Word is simply the story of men and women who decided to live by faith and give glory to God. However, the Lord in His wisdom gave us their stories not only for knowledge but to inspire practical application. In fact, Peter tells us that the Word has given us "all things that pertain to life and godliness" (2 Peter 1:3).

An example of this can be found in James 5, "Elijah was a man with a nature like ours and he prayed that it would not rain; and it did not rain...." James is using the mighty prophet Elijah to communicate that God's adventure is waiting for you by faith.

I have heard it said that our lives are a "tapestry of grace." There are so many different colors and kinds of thread that weave together in order to make a beautiful piece of art. Paul says that we are God's workmanship, and as the Master Designer, He is embroidering every strand of thread within our context to produce in us the incredible image of Jesus.

Lord willing, when we look back at the artwork that has been produced throughout our lifetime, we will see the great story of Christ portrayed in our lives, as we have purposed to reflect His image living by faith and giving glory to God.

As well, God defines Himself as the Potter. Molding and shaping, He takes ordinary pieces of clay and makes extraordinary works of art to be placed on His mantle to reveal His glory. I am sure the clay does not feel great about spinning round and round nor being pressed and squeezed. I am also sure that if the clay could speak, he might say that pulling out all of the unnecessary clay from inside the developing vessel hurts a little.

I know for certain that the pot aches when He is carving and etching His Image on the side. Most especially, I wonder if the vessel is thinking, *Have you lost your mind?* when the kiln is heated in order to secure the form. As a normal piece of clay myself, I understand the plight of the pot.

Our adventure with the Lord is just that. Our stories simply include His knowledge of what He knows we need in order to be conformed into the image of His Son. For some, the stories are simple; for others, they are complex. I am convinced that those who have the latter, as myself, just display how much effort He had to exert to get our attention and cause us to change. It truly is humbling to think that the lessons of faith we should be able to learn in a pew took a war to get across to me.

Those lessons of faith have emerged over my lifetime and experience. Paul was very careful to say in Philippians 3, "Not that I have already attained; but I press on...toward the goal for the prize of the upward call of God in Christ Jesus."

Thus, it is not to say that the lessons have "cured" in my life, but the fire is still heating up and I can be "confident that He who began a good work in me will complete it until the day of Christ Jesus."

There are a few things to keep in mind as I pray you choose to accept your mission. In no way do I assume that these are exhaustive; however, they are simply lessons of faith that I have gained through many trials and errors, successes and failures.

## HONOR GOD!

Adventures are found everywhere. Keep in mind that this is a life-style, not an event. We do not go looking for adventure; we simply purpose to be obedient to everything that God places in front of us. Whether it is at the park with the kids, in line at the grocery store or halfway across the world, there are human beings everywhere that are in need of hearing the gospel of Jesus Christ. Our mission, should we choose to accept it, is to seek and save the lost.

Recently I traveled to London and had to rent a car. Unfortunately, my booking was canceled, and I knew it was going to take a while to rectify the situation because we had already paid for the booking. There were two ladies behind the counter. Over the course of almost two hours, I was able to discuss Jesus with one of the ladies who was a Muslim, as the other woman listened intently (but acted like she was not paying attention).

When the woman with whom I was speaking had to walk out of the office, the other lady whispered to me, "Ok, so you're a pastor! I am a Catholic and am struggling in my faith because of all these bad things that are happening to me."

She went on to explain the crisis of faith she was facing. When the other lady came back, she quickly sat down and acted as if we had not spoken. I played the game. Over the next several minutes as we finished the transaction, I was sure to communicate loud enough the hope of Jesus so that both ladies heard. Adventure!

Several years ago, I was in the Philippines. One of the young men with whom I was traveling was a gymnast and started a small competition of jumps and flips right on the street with some local Filipinos. In about fifteen minutes, there were several hundred people who formed a circle in order to watch these guys perform. In a moment, the Lord gave me a thought...I stepped into the circle and began to preach the gospel.

Adventure!

I like to eat submarine sandwiches. There are a few places that I like to go because the meat is always fresh, the bread is always soft, and the sandwich is always perfect. Two or three times a week, I would visit one of these locations for lunch and found myself engaging in constant conversation with the woman who made my meal. We talked about life. We told stories of our children. She would share her day, and I would tell her about mine. Eventually, I started to pray with her. She came to church and received the Lord. Adventure!

Honoring God is a lifestyle. While I have shared in this section a few triumphant stories of God's grace, in the next section on humility I will share the opposite. The point of the matter is that wherever we go and whatever we do, our lives are to let our light so shine that when men see our good works, they will glorify our Father in heaven.

Mission trips, speaking engagements and events are exciting; however, it is the process of everyday life that prepares us for those occasions. In essence, it is choosing to have the integrity to honor God in all that we say and do, as He is the way, the truth and the life.

The Thessalonians did this well. In the first portion of Paul's letter to this church, he remembers "their work of faith, labor of love and patience of hope in our Lord Jesus Christ in the sight of our God and Father." He commends their testimony of the three things that will remain throughout eternity—faith, hope and love.

Choosing to add to your faith through the Word of God, purposing to live in the hope of Christ's return, and acting in love as the most excellent way is a good, simplistic guide to remember as we choose to honor God.

## HUMBLE YOURSELF!

It is important to note the command in Scripture found in James 4. The apostle writes, "Humble yourselves!" This is not a suggestion. This is not an option. This is a direction.

# IT'S YOUR TURN

We do not have to wonder whether we are prideful or not. We simply have to deal with the fact that we are and purpose to follow this command. Trust me, if we do not deal with it, the Lord will help us because He will not share His glory with another. This lesson was learned early on in my ministry. I was fourteen years old. I had just returned from Africa and was amazed at the reception I received from my home church. People were treating me like a hero. Apparently, the pastor had read one of the letters I wrote home to my parents while I was away and everyone wanted to hear further of the adventures during my time away.

Unfortunately, it all began to go to my head. I started to believe my own press, and before I knew it, I was sharing in the glory of what Christ alone deserves. However, the Scriptures are clear to say, "God opposes the proud and gives more grace to the humble" (1 Peter 5:5).

In only a few weeks, I would come to the full understanding of this text. Our church had a sister church about two hours away. This other church had also sponsored some of my trip financially, and the pastor asked me to come and speak to his congregation of about 500 people on Sunday morning. I was excited about the opportunity to share my testimony but my motives were slightly self-motivated as well.

I will never forget that incredible Sunday morning. I was nervously awaiting my turn to speak. I was sweating and my stomach was in knots. When the pastor called my name, I practically jumped out of my chair before he could finish saying, "Chet Lowe" and was at the podium. Everything seemed to be going great until someone screamed, "He's going down!" In fact, that was the last thing I remembered. I woke up to paramedics poking and prodding me only to realize that I was the person who went down. That's right! I passed out in front of everyone and ended up in the hospital for the rest of the day.

After a full day of a battery of tests, the doctors finally released me with the prognosis of "stage fright" and the direction to go home and get some rest. I was humiliated. What made it worse was that the pastor had asked me to speak that evening at his Sunday night study. My thought was that I could not go in front of those people ever again, yet he insisted, and I obliged.

That night, my tone, my manner and my communication had radically changed. I was humbled before the Lord and would remember this moment for the rest of my life. I am sure each of us has a similar story whereby we have been humbled. Truth is, God will not share His glory with another. Therefore, sometimes I believe that the Lord aids our plight with humility by allowing certain events, people and situations to draw us back to our knees.

In this, prayer is the posture of the humble person. Humility is most reflected in the secret place of our closet, crying out to God for His mercy, power and ability to accomplish the tasks before us. It is the realization of our desperate need to be in constant communication with almighty God for each step we take.

Paul explains it best by saying, "Pray without ceasing." Humility is best practiced when we embrace our weaknesses. We have been born in the flesh. Each of us has issues in our hearts that affect the way we look at life around us. In one sense, they are like filters by which all of life's perspectives pass through to generate an interpretation. Some of those filters are dirty and need to be cleaned. Embracing the fact that we have these weaknesses allows the precepts of the Word to wash the perspective of our thinking so that we can be transformed.

Unfortunately, many people approach life thinking they are right and do not have any broken or dirty filters. They are argumentative, judgmental and oftentimes legalistic. Usually, from their perspective, everyone else has the problem and the world would be a better place if everyone else changed to conform to their way of thinking. In this, you can almost hear the pride of the pharisee in Luke 18. Jesus referenced him as He observed the publican praying in the temple.

From the Pharisee's perspective, his hope was that all men should be as he was. Yet, the only one that was heard by the Lord that day was the publican who embraced his weakness and in humility cried out for forgiveness. It is important to see that the posture of prayer is just as important as the prayer itself.

We must approach God in humility. Humble prayer will keep us from pride because we will constantly be encountering His Presence in front of the glorious throne of grace. It is in this place that our lives will be changed as we plead for mercy, recognizing the pieces of us that must be transformed in the face of God's goodness. Purposing to be continually in His Presence through prayer affords the believer the privilege, like Isaiah, to behold His glory and realize that humility is our only option in light of His magnificence.

## LOVE IS THE MOST EXCELLENT WAY!

I have always been fascinated with the story of Jesus asking Peter if he loved Him. I have heard pastors proclaim that He asked Peter three times because he denied Jesus three times. I have heard it interpreted narratively and allegorically. Yet, with each sermon or devotional moment, I am overwhelmed with the magnitude of this question. This area of Scripture has been called the "Restoration of Peter." Usually, I think of restoration as someone being rebuked for sin and encouraged through the Word for godly living, but Jesus' approach is so different.

He asks, "Do you love me?" He makes this moment so personal. He is intimate and relational. Not only is He asking the question, He is displaying the unconditional love He is demanding. Peter had denied Him. He forsook Him in His greatest time of need. There is a part of me that demands retribution. I know the Word of God says, "'Vengeance is mine, I will repay,' says the Lord" (Romans 12:19).

Sometimes I wished it said, "'Vengeance is mine, I will repay,' says the Lord's servant." However, in this moment, Jesus is seeking to love and be loved. With such a great offense, one would think that there may have been friction or at the very least, some tension. True to the end, Jesus chooses to love.

# LIVING PARABLE

For ten years, I had befriended a young man. In sincerity, I considered him one of my closest comrades in Liberia. We traveled together. We faced opposition together in the war and even risked our lives together. He had made so many sacrifices for me that I, in turn, wanted to do the same for him. Our love for one another as brothers was like Jonathan and David. His greatest desire was to attend a Bible college in the United States. Thus, I had the opportunity to see this dream to fruition and brought him with me to register for a semester while we were home for a break from the mission field. After three weeks, I drove to his house to pick him up for class. When I walked in, there was a small letter on the couch that said, "Brother Chet...."

I could feel my emotions begin to rage. Somehow, I knew this was not good. The letter read, "Dear Brother Chet, I regret to inform you that I have left. I befriended you for ten years so that you would bring me to the States and now I am gone. Your Brother."

It took eight years before I would hear from him again via email. To be honest, I am glad it did. Had I found him or had he come back to me, I think I would have lost my witness due to the hurt in my heart.

Such betrayal! Such deceit!

*I deserved to be mad*, I thought.

I felt justified in my desire for retribution. Thankfully, Jesus worked on my heart for eight years to be able to receive his email of apology and respond with only the grace that Jesus provides in speaking the truth in love.

My point is that there is no situation in which Jesus did not show the love of God. He did not allow any experience to provide the excuse for vengeance. He won Peter over with His love. Because of this, Peter willingly laid down his life for His Savior, who had shown him real love. We love because He first loved us. In essence, love is the most excellent way. No matter who has hurt us or what has happened to us, the way of love should be our guide.

## IT'S YOUR TURN

I have come to know these three principles intimately in my walk—not because I have perfected them, but because they guide me. Paul said he pressed on though he had not yet attained.

This is my goal.

This is my prayer.

In the next adventure that awaits for you and for me, I pray these principles will help lead us into the abundant life God has for each of us. Once again, my prayer is that these stories simply spur your faith into love and good works. My hope is that they create in you a desire to go into your world and bring about change for the gospel.

Allow the Spirit to move you to places you never dreamed of before as you begin your adventure with the Lord. He guarantees you will be in for a ride that is out of this world (pun intended). Most of all, remember to honor God, humble yourself, and that love is the most excellent way.

Chet Lowe was born on September 1, 1970. At the age of seven, Chet began his first ministry—a Vacation Bible School for the neighborhood children right in his parents' garage. From his father and mother, Ira and Pam Lowe, Chet learned the foundational truths of practical Christianity. He has two siblings: Susan and Matthew. Matthew, a naval aviator, died in 2011 when his plane went down. He was only thirty-three years old.

At thirteen, Chet felt God's call on his life. He joined a team of teenagers and traveled to South Korea to build a church. A year later, a new journey took him to Liberia, West Africa, to build a schoolhouse. These trips solidified in his mind his desire to serve the Lord no matter the calling or the place.

For a boy born on the island of Nassau, Bahamas, which is only seven by twenty-one miles, he was ready to "Go into all the world and preach the gospel."

In 1994, Chet married his wife, Andrea, and since then they have dedicated their lives for the sake of God's kingdom. Chet's passion for God's work led him to return to Liberia in 1995, with his wife and their four-month-old child, to minister to the Liberian nation in the middle of a civil war. For several years, he and his family worked diligently to bring peace to the hearts of men in the midst of such turmoil and strife. Threatened with war, ambush, disease and hunger, Chet and his family were able to overcome by the blood of the Lamb and see the fruit of planting seventeen churches.

These churches co-labored with his desire to minister to the children who were fighting in the civil war. Working in conjunction with the local church, he opened seven rehabilitation homes known as Joseph's Brethren. These homes ministered to over 1,500 child soldiers (ages five to eighteen) by taking them out of combat, showing them the love of Christ through a well-structured, six-week ministry and placing them in foster homes until their biological families could be found.

Upon his return to the United States in 2000, Chet joined the staff of his home church of fifteen years, Calvary Chapel Fort Lauderdale. He had the privilege to serve the Lord as the Adult Family pastor and oversee the Couples' Ministry, Pre-Marital and Weddings, Biblical Counseling, Women's Ministry, Free Indeed (a sin deliverance ministry), Singles, Parenting and the Foster Care Ministry.

In 2005, he pioneered a young adult discipleship ministry, which is still in operation and known as Patmos: Reality Discipleship. It has operated since then in several different locations such as Campo Mourao, Brazil; Nassau, Bahamas; and South Florida. Chet served at Calvary Chapel Fort Lauderdale for twenty-seven years and is now co-laboring with Calvary Chapel Costa Mesa and Calvary Chapel South Bay in Southern California.

Chet and his wife are blessed with several children: five through natural birth, three adopted Liberian children and many more sons in the faith. He realizes his family to be his greatest ministry as "to whom much is given, much is required." In the same way, he desires to know Christ better, which has led him to complete his Master's Degree in Christian Counseling.

It is his heartfelt desire to raise up the next generation for Jesus Christ. He believes his calling is to prepare the coming of the Lord by discipling a younger generation to be passionate for Jesus.